A Mother's Heart IV

Edited by Dr. Cassundra White-Elliott

CLF Publishing, LLC.
www.clfpublishing.org
909.315.3161

Copyright © 2019 by Mary Andrews, Edwin Baltierra, Catherine Boshoven, Shelia A. Bryant-Colbert, Ariel Castillo, Jean Cedeno, Caroline Ferrer, Joshua Garza, Yesenia Hernandez, Casey Howard, Jordan Rice, and Christopher Rodriguez.

All rights reserved. No portion of this book may be reproduced, stored in a retrieval system, or transmitted by any form or any means electronically, photocopied, recorded, or any other except for brief quotations in printed reviews, without the prior permission of the publisher.

Cover Design by Senir Design. Contact information- info@senirdesign.com.

ISBN # 978-1-945102-38-7

Printed in the United States of America.

Dedications

This book is dedicated to mothers around the world who take time out of their own lives to nurture, teach, scold, and love the children they are blessed to have (whether they gave birth to them, adopted them, or if God blessed them spiritually with them). May God direct your paths as you interact with your children and may you be encouraged every step of the way.

Acknowledgements

I appreciate each of the contributors to this book. Each story/letter was written with love and respect for a wonderful woman. I thank each of you for your willingness to participate in this book and your adherence to all requests. This book is a success because of you!

Table of Contents

Grandma Linda — 11
    Mary Andrews

Mama Carmen — 19
    Edwin Baltierra

A Light in the Dark — 27
    Catherine Boshoven

A Beautiful Red Rose — 41
    Shelia A. Bryant-Colbert

A Light in My Life — 47
    Ariel Castillo

A Mother in White — 55
    Jean Cedeno

Ana Banana — 65
    Caroline Ferrer

Cherishing You — 71
    Joshua Garza

To A Special Woman — 79
    Yesenia Hernandez

A Dedication to the Strongest Woman	87
Casey Howard	
A Mother with Super Powers	95
Jordan Rice	
Gracias Mamá	107
Christopher Rodriguez	
Gift of Salvation	117
About the Editor	123

Introduction

Mothers around the world have dedicated their lives to their children. They take seriously the task of nurturing, loving, developing, educating, and preparing them for life. However, unbeknownst to most mothers, they face a task that is embedded with many challenges, such as the life of a teenager, rebellion, the terrible two's, etc. Despite the challenges, mothers forge ahead with the task at hand. With the love they have for their children, they endure many hardships, even when the same love is not returned or fully appreciated. They strive to stay focused on the task at hand and refrain from allowing anything to deter them.

On this road of motherhood, women embark upon this journey without a manual. They enter motherhood not fully knowing what to expect from the children they will raise. They don't know what the children's behavior patterns will be, their likes or dislikes, or how they will respond to different life experiences. Motherhood is truly on-the-job training.

Through the joys and pains, through the tears and metaphorical rain, mothers press on. At times, their love is equally reciprocated while at other times it is not. At times, children are found to be treasures, and at other times, they are not. At times, children are found to be obedient, while at other times, they are not. One constant you will find is – regardless of how the children are, mothers would not trade their children in for anything else in the world. Mothers take their children as they are!

Because of this unconditional love, their endurance, and their commitment, mothers are worth their just due. They are worthy of praise, and they are worthy of honor.

In this book, you will read the stories of many mothers written by their children who wanted to honor them. Some of the mothers have passed on, but their memories remain. The other mothers who are being honored are alive and well. They will have the opportunity to read the words their children have written.

Please note- this book is not to paint mothers as saints. It is to show their humanness, their successes and their mistakes, their triumphs and their trials. It is to honor them for all they have done. By no means are mothers perfect, but with their love, they have seen their children through many battles. It is because of who they are/were that we are who we are.

After examining the lives of my grandmother, mother and aunts and being a mother and grandmother myself, I know the sacrifices a mother makes for her children. A mother always wants what is best for her children. She will give them the dress from her back and the food from her plate to make sure her children are well cared for.

As you read through the story of each mother, I want you to think about a mother you know. She may be your mother, your grandmother, your aunt, a friend, a cousin, a sister, a mother-in-law, or a co-worker. As you think about this mother, think about how you can encourage her. Whether you know it or not, mothers need to be encouraged. They need to know that their labor is not in vain.

When my mother was alive, I told her, "Thank you for loving me. Thank you for teaching me. Thank you for placing me above all else. Thank you for being my mother."

Today, I encourage the young mothers in my life. I tell them when they are doing a great job with their children, especially the mother of my grandchildren. Also, I give them pointers (in love) when they can do better. I believe my words encourage them to be tender, loving mothers. As I speak to the young mothers, I must remember that they are relatively new to mothering, and they are learning through the joys and challenges of motherhood, just as I did when raising my two sons.

To all mothers- we cannot change the past. We cannot undo any mistakes we may have made. All we can do is strive for a better tomorrow for ourselves and for our children. Be encouraged! You are not alone in this job of motherhood. There are many mothers who share your concerns, your worries, and your fears.

Motherhood is a joy. Enjoy every moment of your adventure and spend as much time with your children that you can. Love them with all heart, and whether you experience ups and downs or a smooth ride, your children will never forget your love.

Dr. Cassundra White-Elliott

A Mother's Heart IV

Grandma Linda

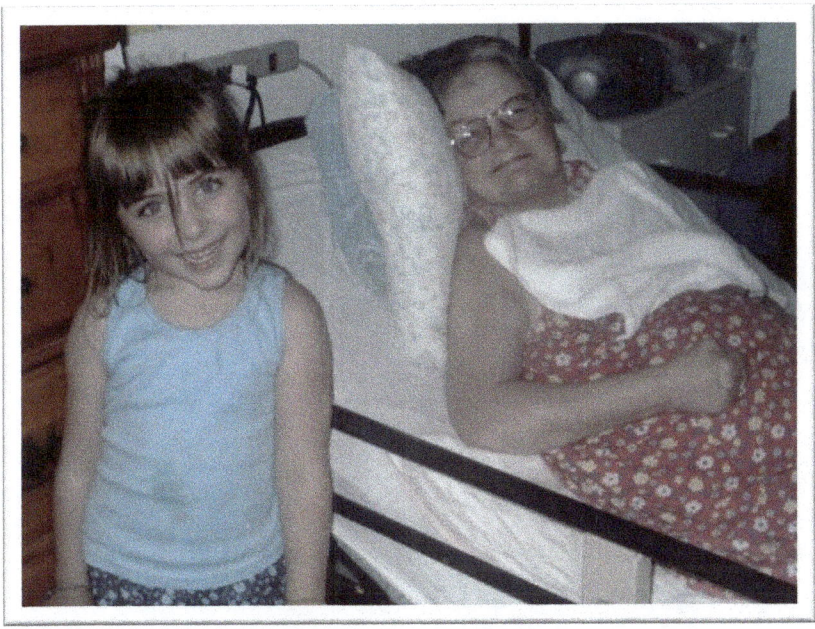

Mary Andrews

Edited by Dr. C. White-Elliott

"There are memories that time does not erase...

Forever does not make loss forgettable, only bearable."

Cassandra Clare, City of Heavenly Fire

A Mother's Heart IV

How am I supposed to start this?

What should I write first?

Either way, this story may end in tragedy. It may make you sad, it may make you teary-eyed like it has me, and I do not think I can avoid that. If I am going to tell you about my grandmother, if I am going to honor her memory - then you should know right now that it ends not as it should.

It ends with her not being alive anymore.

When I was younger, I thought being in your fifties meant you were *old*, but now I understand that is too young to die. It is too young to leave the earth. But, my grandmother had to go anyway, despite all of our protests against it.

I wish I could remember more about her, but even a six year old can only retain so much before some things fade away. There are things in my life now that I have as memoirs of her, i.e. the Polaroid picture of her in my photo album and the thin, white scar below my bottom lip that I got after having a close encounter with the railing on the side of her bed. They still will never be enough.

The loss of my grandmother hurt a lot more when I was younger. For example, on days when I was in middle school and my school would have "Grandparents Day," and all the kids would invite their grandmothers and grandfathers in order to honor them. For me, it was never my grandmother in the stands waving at me as I sang in the fifth grade choir. There were only my mom and dad present. They were the backup actors, the ones that stepped in when the real deal could not. And my real deal could not.

Even now though, I feel her absence at nineteen years old.

But I do not want to talk about the things she had to miss since her passing. I want to talk about what I saw of her and what I remember of her, even if it is such a small fraction of the woman she was.

The stories I heard of my grandma Linda growing up all came from her daughter, my mom. She used to tell me that when I was born, I brought a little bit more life into my grandmother's life, because it was like my mom was a baby all over again. I also know that if she were alive right now, I would be swimming in the gifts and things she would buy me. She was a bit of a shopaholic. It makes me laugh when I think about it.

I also know that my grandmother was probably the funniest and sassiest woman ever. It is what the women in my family pass down: humor, sass, and a whole lot of cuss words. So, my grandmother was not the most lady-like. I have a picture I recently received from my mom, and it is of my grandmother at a wedding. All you can see is the back of her, with her arms high up in the air as she danced. I do not think she was supposed to be the subject of the picture, but she captured all the attention.

I do remember her though, even if it is only fractures of memories in my brain. I remember the time I opened one of the cabinets in her room and found a pretty pink Hello Kitty blanket she had gotten for me. Turns out, it was a present, and I was definitely not meant to see it. Her eyes got really big when I squealed out, "Hello Kitty!"

I remember all the times I sat on the feet of her automatic wheelchair, and we would go around the parking lot in circles over and over. It was enough that I even got my own little pillow.

A Mother's Heart IV

I remember the Wednesdays after school when my mom and I would visit her. I would sit on the bed across from hers that was always strangely empty and eat the grilled cheese sandwiches she had. Turns out, I was eating her dinner, but she never even told me. So, I would munch away on her food without a care in the world.

I remember her voice, and how I was so *amazed*, because it felt like my mom was the only one who could really understand her. It was as though they had their own language. If she were alive now, I think I would know that language too.

I remember her hair, her face, and how she smelled. Or maybe, that was just the place she lived in. Maybe, it was both.

And, I remember the night when my mom and I were at home, watching a movie, and my mom got a call. I do not know how, but the second that phone rang, I knew what had happened.

I remember my mom crying a simple, "No." And all my fears were confirmed. That was when my own memories of her would cease to be made.

I wish I had more reminders of her; I wish I could write pages and pages about "I remember we did this," and "I remember this one time. . ." But I cannot, and that is something I cannot change in this life. It is hard knowing I will never have her around. She did not get to see me graduate high school or go on to start college. She did not see me get a short story published for the first time, and she never got to meet my boyfriend. She would have liked him though. He would have made her laugh.

I love her a ton. It is a relationship no back up actor can replace. I am going to think of her every time I push my tongue against the inside of my bottom lip and my scar becomes apparent. I am going to think of her every time I see my friends with their grandparents. I am going to think of her, and what we had, and what we did not. I cherish what we did have, though.

I am *proud* she is my grandmother.

Writing this has not been the easiest thing, because even now I know she will not be able to read it. But, I believe she knows.

Somehow.

One day, I will get to see her again, and I will tell her everything I have been able to do and some of the things I have not yet accomplished. I will hear her talk, and her language will be the same as mine. I will hug her hard. I will see her walk. Until then, I will keep on remembering her, honoring her, and loving her - even if life and death is the bridge between us.

About the Author

Mary Andrews is currently enrolled in her second year at Crafton Hills College where she is majoring in English, American Sign Language, and Humanities. Her passion for writing has taken her to be previously published in *The Christmas Mosaic II*. She was also published in the *Palouse Review* in December 2018 for her photography. Her goals are now to go on to get her Master's degree in English at the University of Idaho and explore her options as an author.

Edited by Dr. C. White-Elliott

A Mother's Heart IV

MAMA CARMEN

Edwin Baltierra

Edited by Dr. C. White-Elliott

Happy Mother's Day to all the wonderful mothers

out there who make a difference every day,

by working hard for their families.

My story is about my amazing grandmother Carmen Baltierra. Mama Carmen was born on March 10, 1929, in the suburbs, right outside of Mexicali. Unfortunately, she passed away November 2015 due to cancer. She was always a strong woman and never showed her weakness to anyone. Mama Carmen was the best grandmother anyone could have ever asked for. She was a very loving human being.

Ever since I can remember, my dearest grandmother was nothing but a joy! I have never felt the amount of love I felt from her from anyone else. Mama Carmen was someone I could always go to for advice, love, and happiness. Whenever I had a bad day or week, I would speak to her and my entire mood would instantly become better. It is fair enough to say that Mama Carmen was a saint. That woman was pure and good. There was never one day in my entire life that I witnessed her become upset at someone or something. Growing up in the United States and having my grand-mother live in a different country was very difficult as a young kid. Because of the distance, I was not always able to speak to my grandmother whenever I wanted to. And, I had to wait until we had a family trip to Mexicali in order to visit her.

As a young child, visiting my grandmother's home was the most amazing time of my life. I remember all the crazy adventures I went on with my siblings in my grandmother's backyard. Her backyard was huge and filled with tall trees and beautiful plants and flowers everywhere.

Mama Carmen always had delicious food prepared for anyone at any time. She was a woman who loved to feed everyone! I can recall always waking up to her delicious homemade flour tortillas and fresh beans with cheese and avocado each morning. It was so delicious! That was the usual breakfast at any Mexican home out there.

She was always the happiest when all her babies were sitting at her table, eating together as one. It is very traditional for a Mexican family to do this because mealtime goes beyond just eating; we all bond together and enjoy each other's company in the ways our ancestors taught us.

Mama Carmen was the type of grandma to sneak up on me when I was sleeping and add an extra pillow underneath my head and blanket on top of me. Sleeping at her house was never a night too cold or too hot. She always took good care of me.

Mama Carmen always put everyone first before herself. She was never selfish. She only taught us how to love each other and the importance of staying united as a family. In her eyes, I know she was very proud and happy of the family she had created. She felt blessed and thanked God every single day of her life.

As I grew older, I turned into something I wasn't entirely proud of. I began to dislike traveling to Mexicali. It was not that I did not like my family anymore; it was just the horrible traffic and time it took to get back home. The constant traveling turned from a luxury to an inconvenience for me. I understand my parents one hundred percent for never getting tired of visiting Mexico. They grew up there, and they love their home. That is why I never question anything that my parents do because, as their son, I have to respect whatever they want.

A Mother's Heart IV

Looking back to the days that my grandmother was still alive, I felt very selfish and guilty. I have been very unhappy with myself simply because I know I wasn't there enough for my grandmother. I let my stupidity get to me, and I never thought of her. My grandmother dreamed of my siblings and me visiting her, but we would only think of ourselves and never think of her first. I was so disappointed at what I had become because that is not what she thought of my siblings and me.

When we received the news that she was diagnosed with cancer, we obviously became very emotional and wanted to see her immediately. In the back of my mind, I almost did not want to go because at that point, I felt as if I was a hypocrite for showing up then after hardly ever visiting her. My parents understood completely what I said to them, and they advised me that it was never too late to visit Grandma, but it was very important to do it then because she only had a few months left to live.

When I found out my grandmother only had a few months left to live, my head completely blacked out. I was frozen. I had no idea what to do or say. I couldn't even cry because I was still in shock. In my mind, my grandmother was always going to be there because she was always very healthy and never got sick. That woman had never touched a cigar in her entire life! Hearing that my grandmother had been diagnosed with cancer was so unexpected and unheard of. Everyone was surprised and heartbroken.

Soon after, we drove out to Mexicali to visit her and see how she had been doing. Once we arrived to the hospital, we went up to her room, and we finally saw her again. Instead of visiting her at home and at her very finest, we went there to see her suffering and very depressed. As soon as we walked in and made eye contact with her, a huge bright smile appeared on her face. That made me want to tear up so badly inside because of all the guilt I had, but I had to hold it in.

Seeing Mama Carmen smile at me made me realize how blessed I have been my entire life with a beautiful angel like her. I felt as though I had disappointed her, but I knew she still loved me and understood why I acted the way I did. I had never before seen my grandmother hospitalized and hardly breathing. That was so hard for me to process because I had to understand that my momma was going to die soon. It was so painful to see her in that position, but seeing her big smile made everything feel much better. Her smile showed me how strong and powerful she was. That's the Mama Carmen that I had known and loved since I was a little boy.

All I can say to my grandma now is that I love her very much, and I am very sorry for everything that happened. I am sorry for not being there enough, especially when she needed me the most. I hate the fact that she had to go that way, but I know she is in a much better place now. Words cannot express enough the love I have for my grandmother. I think of her every single day, and I always have her in my heart. I know she is in heaven, watching over my family and me. I know she is no longer suffering anymore.

A Mother's Heart IV

May God always bless my little angel from above and give her nothing but paradise. I love you!

Te quiero mucho, Mama Carmen.

Tu hijo
-Winnie

Edited by Dr. C. White-Elliott

About the Author

    Edwin Baltierra is a full-time college student at College of the Desert, in the Coachella Valley, and a full-time makeup artist at Bobbi Brown. He is currently double majoring in journalism and audio production in hopes of becoming an entertainment reporter and have his own talk show or becoming a well-known and successful music producer. Edwin Baltierra is also pursuing a solo artist career and dancing career as soon as he graduates with his first degree. Edwin has paused chasing his musician dreams because of school. Mr. Baltierra does not want to look back in ten years and not have at least one degree from a university, especially since he will be the first in his family to receive one. Laughter, dancing, singing, and having lots of fun is an everyday ritual in Edwin Baltierra's life. He does not believe in a dull moment, so joking around is always the best way to cheer up and make life a little easier and fun.

A Mother's Heart IV

A Light in the Dark

Catherine Boshoven

Edited by Dr. C. White-Elliott

Daffodowndilly

She wore her yellow sun-bonnet,
She wore her greenest gown;
She turned to the south wind
And curtsied up and down.
She turned to the sunlight
And shook her yellow head,
And whispered to her neighbor:
"Winter is dead."

A. A. Milne

A Mother's Heart IV

Mothers have one of the most difficult jobs in the world: raising the generation to come. They are responsible for caring for the people who will set the course for the future. That comes with a lot of pressure and responsibility, and it's no easy thing. Raising a child is a one-way ticket to the unknown, and mothers don't always get credit for it. They get a pat on the back once in a while when their kid keeps quiet during dinner in a restaurant. But what about the times when the kid isn't so quiet? What about the times when the mother gently corrects her child about something he/she is doing, and in response, the mother is met with a temper-tantrum? What about all the hours spent cooking for the child, cleaning up each mess, and waking up in the night to attend to the child's request for a drink of water?

The saddest part is, the children don't realize just how much their mom sacrifices for them until much later in life, and even when they grow older, they don't always take the time to show thanks. Looking back over the years of my life, I see just how much my mother has sacrificed for me, and I strive to thank her as often as I can (though it's not nearly often enough), because like many of my peers, I never realized it when I was young.

Growing up in a house in the mountains, my family was very detached from the rest of bustling California. Grocery trips were special events reserved for Fridays, and winters were spent building snowmen on the driveway or huddling beside the fireplace to keep warm. Some days, the snow would be so deep that it was impossible for my dad to drive to work, and he would spend the morning plowing the snow from the driveway with my mom beside him with the shovel.

Luckily for my siblings and me, my mom homeschooled us, so we didn't have to worry about getting to school through the snow or spending our days outdoors in the cold months of fall and winter. On the other hand, we weren't a slacking homeschooling family either, where the work never gets done and the television is always on. My mom woke us up early every morning for breakfast and devotions, and she faithfully taught us throughout the day all the subjects required by established schools. She typed up schedules for each day, organized our subjects into specific time periods, and taught each of us what we needed to know. Her entire life was consumed with giving us the education we needed, and only looking back now do I realize just how much time and energy she put into teaching us.

But despite the heavy workload, she enjoyed every bit of it. She taught us the names of the kings of ancient Israel and Judah, the letters of the Greek and Hebrew alphabets, the last names of all the presidents of the United States, and even the names of all the kings and queens of England. She had us memorize short Bible verses that I will automatically pull from my memory in times of need, and she memorized it all right along with us to help us remember. She also relearned math to help my sister and me understand the complicated equations that made absolutely no sense to either of us.

We got a good education in science as well, which my mother will say herself is no favorite of hers. The older of my two younger brothers has always wanted to be a veterinarian like my dad, and she read specified books with him and helped him with assignments, even when it held no interest for her. She organized a weekly science lab with some friends to give all of us the opportunity to learn about dissection and different chemical changes, and when it came to anything concerning science, she tried her best to answer all of our questions—and my brother had a lot of those—to give us the facts we needed when looking at the world from a scientific viewpoint. That meant taking us on nature hikes, memorizing all the bones in the body, and looking up funny rhyming videos on the elements in the periodic table.

Best of all, she thoroughly taught us how to write. Having received a Bachelor's Degree in English, she was more than qualified to teach us the art of writing, and she never ran out of ideas for lessons or books for us to read. I think my favorite memory of those homeschooling times was when she read to us. At the end of every school day, she would gather us into the sitting room and read us a book, whether it was *Holes, The Cat of Bubastes, The Tales of Prydain,* or *Children of the New Forest.* She even read us many of Shakespeare's plays, including *Much Ado About Nothing*, which is a favorite of mine. When we got older, she had us read with her in a reader's theater setting, and of those books, the most memorable to me was the Harry Potter series. Since there were so many characters, it gave all of us a chance to refine our reading skills.

All of the books she read to us are like shining lights in my mind. There is nothing like a story read to you in childhood. It influences your life and views of the world in ways that are indescribable. I still remember the eloquent writing of those authors and the beautiful outlook they had on life in the stories they wove. I remember every voice my mother used to bring the stories to life and every face she drew to represent the many characters in various books, so my youngest brother could understand better. The readings gave me more of an education in books than I think I ever would have received elsewhere.

At the end of every school year, she would have my siblings and me choose one person in our lives—family or close friend—to come over for a special event on the last day of school. The four of us kids would sing a song together as an opening, while she accompanied on the piano, and then we would repeat all of the memorization work we had learned. Then, we would individually show our chosen person the various geography maps we had drawn, the monthly projects we had put together for science, and all the essays we had written on books and historical events. It was our end-of-year test, so to speak, which taught me in more ways than memory.

I learned speaking and writing skills, and it gave me a confidence I never would have received anywhere else: a confidence to outdo myself. My mother taught me that the only competition I should be concerned about is myself. The only person I should constantly try to beat is myself. This changed my view on many different aspects of life, especially writing. I was very young when I realized how wondrous writing is, and I spent much of my free-time writing down the dreams and ideas always swirling in my head. And although most of the writings were pathetic little scribblings created by a twelve-year-old, my mom sat beside me and read every single page. She read my stories with the eye of an editor and the heart of a true admirer.

I wrote page after page of useless fantasies, and she found ways to compliment them, encouraging me to continue writing and enhance my skills. She asked me questions about the little worlds I had created, showing me—with great patience—every grammar mistake, and any time I compared myself to Tolkien or Jane Austin, she gently guided my attention back to myself, telling me the only work I should be worried about was my own. She taught me to believe in my writing, even when I looked at it with despair.

Now when I write, I don't compare myself to other writers. I look at my writing with a critical eye, just as she taught me, so I can find the weaknesses and improve where needed. The greatest skill I learned was the ability to self-criticize, which is a very valuable skill indeed.

Years passed, our homeschooling progressed, and my parents made the decision to move off the mountain. That was a big step for all of us, changing our lives completely. The most obvious change to my siblings and me was the large amount of people that entered our everyday lives. The spaces between houses were so small compared to the expanse of forest between houses in the mountains, and wandering wasn't quite legal anymore. There were no climbing-worthy trees, and the only fireplaces in the house were electronic. However, with the downsides came the upsides as well. The grocery store was only ten minutes away, and our church had many more children our age. The house was also much warmer during the winters, and there were outdoor pools in the community. Our social circles expanded in ways none of us kids even imagined, and our lives became like the families on tv—we even had a mailbox.

Not too long after we had moved to the flat land of California, my sister and I joined a youth theater program. Because we had grown up singing with our brothers and mom, the program sounded very exciting, and my mom agreed to let us join. It was very difficult for her, however, because the program was located an hour away—sometimes two—from our home. The drives were long and taxing, and gas and food expenses were no small thing. But regardless of the energy and time it took, my mom never failed to take us to the countless rehearsals and shows. She even volunteered as a stage manager, giving even more energy and time to the program as a whole.

All the kids in the program adored her, too, which shouldn't have been a surprise. She was always willing to help, even if she had to sacrifice her own personal time for it. She attended extra rehearsals in order to memorize the many ques she had to call, and she never slacked on her duties during the long hours of each show. She even complimented the kids performing after they had finished a particularly hard dance routine or song. She was a shining light to all the kids in that theater program, and when we left, they were very sad to see her go.

But change happens sooner or later, and when my older sister graduated from high school—and thus the theater program—we moved on to the next phase of our lives. Although it was sad to leave the program, theater had always been my sister's passion, not mine, and my mom and I decided it was best for us to leave and focus on activities closer to home. In addition, the older of my younger brothers was to be a freshman in high school, and because he was still very determined in his goal to be a veterinarian, my parents decided a private school would be our next step in life. The work my mom had done in homeschooling had prepared us for so much, giving us the tools we needed to learn about the world around us in a lasting way, but the science books my mom read to us could only teach us so much, and she wanted us to attend classes taught by professional teachers who had gone to college to specifically teach science and advanced math. To make that happen, she started looking for a job to help with the expected payments of private school.

It wasn't long before one private school in particular gave her an interview straight off the bat, seeming very eager to hire her as their new English teacher. As a package deal, my brothers and I would go to the school for free if my mom accepted the position. This was the deal our family had only been dreaming of, and after some prayer and thought, my mom accepted the job. At the time, we had no clue as to the reasons behind the school's desperation in hiring on such short notice, nor did we question the strange luck of the amazing deal. We walked onto campus the first day of school with bright smiles and warm greetings, never expecting what was to follow.

We hadn't reached three months into the semester before the school started to show its true colors. For starters, there was a serious lack of proper facilities. High schoolers had to share a small campus with the preschoolers, and the middle school campus was located across the street in a church. The bathrooms were a horror like none other, and the seating for lunch was outdoors, which was very unfortunate for us students during the cold and rainy months of fall and winter. As the year continued, things only grew worse.

Members of the staff were randomly fired, substitutes came and went, and a few months after the second semester started, teachers stopped receiving paychecks. Once the teachers stopped getting paid, the students and faculty realized as a whole that the school was truly falling apart. It was a hard punch in the gut for all of us. Teachers stopped showing up for work, students' grades started dropping, and management detached themselves as much as they could for the sake of their own preservation. It was only a matter of time until it all crumbled, and with how quickly things were moving, it would be sooner rather than later.

However, despite all of the trials that bombarded our lives and the lives of the other families and students, my mom carried on through it all. No one prayed as fervently as she did; no one attended school as often as she did; no one worked as hard as she did, even when the paychecks stopped coming. No matter how much I begged her to give up and not attend school so diligently, she never gave in. No matter how many problems there were, she never gave up. I grew tired of putting on the uniform and striving to keep a smile on my face, but she marched to school every single day and helped all of those around her make it through the trials. She hadn't given up, even when many of us had. She taught us all with unfailing strength, making sure to give her kids—students and family alike—the education she felt we deserved.

She helped us bring our grades up while teaching us how to work hard for what we wanted, and she prayed with us every single morning. She read to us until her voice was gone, and then she read some more, and as trying as the situation was, she pushed us through with the patience and strength we desperately lacked. She made her classroom a safe haven in that school, and when the year finally came to an end, we came out all the better for it. No matter how far we all went after that, moving on to new schools and better circumstances, none of us would forget the brilliant ray of hope my mom was in our lives during that dark school year.

My junior year of high school would've been worthless without my mom's stubbornness in pushing me through, and I know most of her students would say the same thing. Her students adored her, just as the kids in the theater program had, and it was eye-opening. It was about a year later that my mom and I attended a football game of one of the schools most of her students had transferred to. I had expected the evening to be somewhat uneventful, with a few greetings and some hugs here and there. But I didn't expect the students to flock to my mom, begging to talk to her and share their recent life events. I saw her surrounded by a circle of students, with smiles beaming, and I realized just how special she had become to them.

I can't even describe the pride I felt for my mom in that moment. She had managed to win the hearts of multiple high school sophomores and juniors, so much so that the moment she was first spotted at the game, word of her arrival spread like wildfire. She had been the mother-figure these students had needed to get through the trials of that horrible school year, and no one would ever be able to take that away from them.

The memories we share of her class are permanent beacons in our minds. We will remember the ridiculous games we would play in class and how desperate she was to get us to be friends and interact with each other. We will remember the constant reprimanding regarding curse words and inappropriate talk and the even more constant vocabulary quizzes that never seemed to end. We will remember the timed journal entries she had us write every single day to increase our handwriting speed. She graded every single entry and would even remember the smallest details from those entries when talking to us. She knew us better than we knew ourselves, and she never ceased to direct us in the right direction.

Seeing her surrounded by the kids that adored her, I suddenly saw her for who she truly was and is: a woman who sacrificed for the sake of others. I began to remember the countless books she read to me, the countless hour-long trips out to the youth theater program, and the countless hugs she gave me whenever I left her classroom at school. I began to remember the days she spent grading my stories and discussing my newest idea for a novel, and the different dinners we made together, so I could learn how to cook. I began to remember the multiple bits of wisdom she always gave me, and the ridiculous song she would sing when waking my siblings and me up every morning for school, which came to be so annoying but so endearing at the same time.

It pained me to know that it took me that long to realize just how much my mother has done for me. My entire perspective changed, and I am so thankful for that. She wasn't the overprotective mother that never failed to correct my grammar anymore. She was and is a glowing lantern, my light in the darkness, showing the way home and directing me back to the right path. I know now that I am the person I am today because of her constant guidance and love. I now see her to be the diligent teacher, the faithful friend, and the loving mother she had always been and always will be for me, and I couldn't be more blessed to have her as my mother.

Edited by Dr. C. White-Elliott

About the Author

Catherine Boshoven is a high school student attending college classes at Crafton Hills Community College and taking online courses through Sage Oak Charter Schools. She lives in Highland, California, with her family, working part-time in childcare. She plans to attend Crafton Hills Community College full-time in the 2019 Fall semester to pursue an AA in English. Her ultimate goal is to transfer to a UC to receive a BA in English for the purpose of becoming a book editor. She spends her free time writing short stories and reading novels. She also enjoys exploring the art of cooking and playing the piano.

A Mother's Heart IV

A Beautiful Red Rose

Shelia Ann Bryant-Colbert

Edited by Dr. C. White-Elliott

F is for Flexibility

L is for Loving

O is for Outgoing

W is for Wisdom

E is for Energetic

R is for Reliable

A Mother's Heart IV

To my mother Billie Jean Bryant Alexander, whom I love dearly.

My mother reminds me of a beautiful red rose. She has a soft touch, but also a few thorns. She stands strong in what she believes, like a palm tree that never bends to the ground but always bounces back.

Watching my mother going through her illness and trusting the Lord to bring her through let me know that whatever we're going through, we can trust God. He is who He says He is. Her favorite scripture is Isaiah 54:17: *"No weapon formed against you shall prosper, and every tongue which rises against you in judgment you shall condemn. This is the heritage of the servants of the Lord, and their righteousness is from Me, says the Lord."*

I thank the Lord for my mother. When I lost my husband Rodney, she stayed with me, praying for me, holding my hand, and letting me know the Lord would give me strength. In doing that, I made it through. My mother is the greatest mother, grandmother, and great grandmother. Most of all, she is my best friend. I am so glad that God has blessed me with a beautiful flower forever and always. I love you, Mother. Forever!

Billie, this is for you: *"Sing to the Lord with grateful praise; make music to our God on the harp. He covers the sky with clouds; he supplies the earth with rain and makes grass grow on the hills. He provides food for the cattle and for the young ravens when they call. His pleasure is not in the strength of the horse, nor his delight in the legs of the warrior; the Lord delights in those who fear him, who put their hope in his unfailing love. Extol the* LORD, *Jerusalem; praise your God, Zion. He strengthens the bars of your gates and blesses your people within you"* (Psalm 147:7-13, NIV).

Your daughter,
Shelia

About the Author

Shelia Ann Bryant-Colbert is a mother of three and a grandmother of seven. She is blessed to still have her mother, who is seventy-six years old, with her. Shelia governs her life by the Word of God and strives to live a balanced life between family, church and career. For twenty-five years, she has cared for hospice patients and continues to look forward to doing it daily. She cherishes the time she spends with her grandchildren. She delights in being influential in their lives and speaking the Word of God to them.

Edited by Dr. C. White-Elliott

A Mother's Heart IV

THE LIGHT OF MY LIFE

Ariel Castillo

Edited by Dr. C. White-Elliott

All that I am, or hope to be, I owe to my angel mother.

Abraham Lincoln

A Mother's Heart IV

What makes a mother? Well, the idea of a mother is universal. However, everyone has a different perspective on what defines a mother. Personally, a mother is someone who encourages you to pursue your dreams, picks you back up when you are at your lowest, and believes in you unconditionally, even when you don't believe in yourself. My mother fits all of these categories and more. She is one of the most prominent people in my life; I have no clue what I would do without her!

My mother was born and raised in war-torn Nicaragua. As a Nicaraguan growing up during a time of civil war, she experienced many traumatic experiences that to this day continue to impact her. She had a rough life in her country, having experienced war first-hand and witnessing countless deaths, pain and suffering. She saw things no child should ever have to endure. She and her mother (my grandmother) were in fact nearly killed by rebel forces. Buses carrying school children were set afire. Citizens unlucky to be in the path of traveling forces were killed for no reason, having their properties taken and used by them. My mother's younger brother had to be hidden to avoid being forcibly taken and made to fight. It made life for her and her family tremendously terrifying.

Due to these experiences, she became very appreciative of life and the family she had. She realized not many people in her country were as lucky as she was to be alive and survive. She enjoyed school but could not always remain, as her family needed help. Therefore, she became independent and a hard worker at a young age. She made countless sacrifices, which she found necessary. Like any child, all she wanted was a happy and fulfilling life-free from strife. Through the grace of God, she, her brother, and mother all made it to the United States to forge a better life despite many obstacles. Then, while in her early twenties, she met and married my father and started a family.

When I was a child, she taught me to appreciate the life I was given and opportunities many Americans take for granted, such as a proper education. She would tell me stories and explained how some people weren't fortunate to live the life I'm living. She never sugarcoated reality but always wanted me to remember that life is what we make it to be. As long as we give it our all and never give up, then our lives will be truly fulfilling.

Growing up, art became a hobby I had a developing passion for. You could say I came out the womb with a pencil because I was always drawing wherever and whenever. It wasn't until I attended middle school that I realized what I truly wanted to be in life: an animator and character designer. Disney was a huge influence in this career choice, but seeing how difficult it is to be a part of this empire, I began to feel discouraged.

When I told my mother how I felt about wanting to be a part of the film industry but felt I wouldn't be a good fit, she told me I have just as good a chance to get in and succeed. She has always encouraged me to always dream big and to use my imagination. Ever since that day, she has been my number one supporter and has continued to encourage me every step of the way.

Being able to be comfortable talking to her about anything is a blessing to me. If I am not doing well in a class or if I feel uncomfortable about a situation that occurred, she is the first person I talk to. In our household, she encourages us to talk to her whenever we may feel alone or when we feel emotional. No matter the situation, she wouldn't dare to berate us or put us down. Although she can be stern depending on what happened, she will always assure us that everything will be alright in the end, and she will help come up with a solution. I've had friends who wish they could be as open with their feelings to their parents as I am with my mother. Although I wish everyone got to experience the reassurance from their parents, I consider myself to be incredibly lucky to have a mother who is so understanding and continues to keep supporting me. Her support means the world to me.

Although there were times where she gave tough love and made everything seem difficult, I really appreciated how she still challenged me to go the distance. She would continue to believe in me when I doubted myself. If I wasn't doing well in a class or had trouble on an assignment, she would be the first person to offer a helping hand to make sure I was on the right path where I needed to be.

Not many people are as fortunate as I to experience this much support from their parents, let alone hear the words "Good job," or "I'm so proud of you!" I've had friends come up and tell me they wished their parents encouraged them or even told them how good of a job they were doing. It's little things such as this that make me realize how lucky I am to have such a wonderful mother who will go the extra mile for me. It's something that I will never take for granted...

Mom, thank you for playing a huge role in my life and for putting up with my shenanigans! I know I can sometimes be a handful for you, but trust me when I say there's no other person I'd rather have as my mother than you. You were always there to give me kisses and loving hugs whenever I needed you, putting my needs before your own. You've always made sacrifices for our family, demonstrating how much of a pillar of strength you are. You're the glue that holds this family together with your endless amount of love. Without you, I would not be where I am today. I would be completely lost without you. Happy Mother's Day, Mom! Thank you so much for all that you do and more. You've given me the most precious gift anyone could ever give: love!

About The Author

Ariel Castillo is an aspiring artist from Redlands, California. She has won awards for the Lions Flag Day writing contest by the San Gabriel Taiwanese Lion Club, Outstanding Language Arts/Writing, and Outstanding Student in Advanced Studio Art. She loves to draw whatever comes to mind and create stories of her own. All mediums are of interest and used for her works. In the future, she hopes to achieve her dream occupation as an animator and character designer at Disney.

Edited by Dr. C. White-Elliott

A Mother's Heart IV

The Mother in White

Jean Cedeno

Edited by Dr. C. White-Elliott

If Nature smiles -- the Mother must

If Nature smiles -- the Mother must
I'm sure, at many a whim
Of Her eccentric Family --
Is She so much to blame?

Emily Dickinson

A Mother's Heart IV

A large kind-hearted woman in a gorgeous white wedding dress walks up to her groom and marries him for eternity. The groom is much older than she and much wiser.

That was the dream my mother had prior to the day she found out my aunt had liver cancer. Then, my uncle shared with us his dream of being at a funeral back in Nicaragua, and a man was warning him that his mother had died and was shown a large woman in a casket. He claimed with anger that she wasn't his mother, but the other man claimed she was his mother over and over again until my uncle woke up.

My family has had past circumstances in which their symbolic dreams would later become reality, and in those two dreams, my aunt who was in a white wedding dress with an unknown groom signified she was ready for the union with the Heavenly Father. My uncle's dream was a very direct and blunt warning. However, because my aunt was a type of a maternal figure, the apparition warned that his mother was in the casket rather than his sister.

My aunt Chepa was a child of God, a wife of a pastor, and a mother to everyone. She was a mother to me, to my aunts and uncles, and to my cousins, nieces and nephews. While she always took care of us, her love and kindness were not just reserved for us. She also cared for others, regardless of whether they were family or not. Unfortunately, during my last visit to Nicaragua, she started feeling ill. However, we were unaware of her being ill, so my aunt, mother and I walked to her house to search for her because we had not seen her for several weeks, and we were pretty concerned for her.

The time I will never forget is the day we went to Jinotepe, Nicaragua, because we were getting ready to have an opportunity to visit her. She was outside manually washing her fourteen-year-old son's clothes, and she dropped everything to give me a hug and offered me a seat. She gave me a large orange bin to sit on because she could not afford decent chairs.

She offered me some soda and some Gallo Pinto, and even though her food was very delicious, I refused. I refused because I dislike taking someone else's food, but she would even cook the nastiest beans and still make them delicious. She was a very humble woman who lived in a house with no doors and a small radio to entertain herself. She did not desire anymore earthly wealth and did not desire any less, because she knew her earthly wealth was only a loan that the Heavenly Father had given her.

It was very recently when our Father decided to collect the loan she borrowed from Him and take her to paradise. Not once she went against His will, and she never disrespected Him or blamed Him for her situation with her health. Just as she was always loyal to our All Mighty God, He was also constantly there for her through her situation.

While my aunt was quickly advancing through the stages of cancer, my mother decided to go to help take care of her. So, she bought a ticket to go by plane because of the grand distance between California and Nicaragua. She landed in San Salvador to stay a night there because the plane landed very late and the other one had left before my mother arrived.

The next morning, she left straight to Managua, Nicaragua where she found our family members waiting for her arrival. They took her straight to the hospital of Jinotepe, where she found my aunt in poor condition. She quickly gave her a long hug and tried comforting her and my eighty-one year old grandmother who was sleeping in the hospital bed.

The minute after she hugged her sister, my aunt told her to go back home because she already saw her, and she could lose her job for coming there. At that time, my aunt was still able to talk and express the pain she was feeling. However, that would not be the case soon. She would not sleep for days because of the pain she felt in her head. She described her pain, and she also described herself being in a large church worshipping the Lord. She told my mother it felt like a party, and she felt comforted by it.

During her last three days, she described to everyone the three men in white clothing who had been visiting her and telling her that she was okay and that soon she would be home. She told her son that she was okay and that soon she would go home, and everything would be fine.

On the last day of her beautiful life, she was unable to speak and was covered with bruises. Her feet were very swollen, and they had turned a dark purple. The doctors were considering amputating them because of the diabetes. She was constantly uncomfortable and screaming from the pain in her head. Her last day was December 24, 2015, and on that day, they brought a second doctor, who was also a pastor, but in a separate church. He took a look at her and said, "I'm sorry, brothers and sisters. Her situation looks harsh; either God cures her on this side or He cures her in transition." He then went to her while she was calmly asleep and started to pray for her. He asked God to finish His will and to allow my aunt to rest. At 12:01 on December 25, she passed away, just as the Christmas fireworks went off. Her heart stopped, and she lost her breathing.

Regardless of her tragic illness, she was a blessed woman. Friends and family, and even strangers from other churches, had visited her. During her earlier days in the hospital, groups from various churches came from different parts of the country, and they all started praying for her. In the United States of America, I was here in California getting two Baptist churches to pray for my aunt, and they both did as best as they could. My friend and I were planning to ask for a prayer blanket on Sunday and send it on Monday, but unfortunately, she passed away before we could ask. The day after my friend and I planned to ask for a prayer cloth, I became terribly sad, and I felt like the world was coming to an end. I became distant and shut down from everyone around me, and I didn't know why.

That afternoon, I went to see a play about the birth of our Savior, and although it did raise my level of hope, I was still very sad. I went to sleep very early on the floor where I had always slept for various years, and I woke up from a dream of my aunt staring at me from a distance in a wedding dress. The dream gave me real anxiety, and I started to freak out in my sleep until I woke up at 11:01, the time she passed away. Nicaragua is an hour ahead of California, so when I woke up it was 11:01, but in Nicaragua it was 12:01.

I fell asleep all over again, and when I anxiously got up at 5 o'clock in the morning, my uncle was already there. He told me that he didn't want to tell us the night before over the phone, so he told us in the morning that at 12:01 on Christmas day my aunt had passed away. When I saw him that early in the morning, I knew right then that my aunt went to cook for our Lord and Savior, but emotionally it still had not hit me, until I saw the video of the funeral.

I saw the video after my mother came back to the United States of America. But before she came home, she was able to find out more about what happened prior to my aunt's hospitalization. My grandmother needed medication, because she suffered from high blood pressure and diabetes. So, my mother went to the local pharmacy to get some medication and to grab some air and to relax from the unfortunate situation.

She walked composedly to the pharmacy, and when she got there, the pharmacist asked my mother, "How is your sister doing? Is she better?" My mother grievously had to explain to her that my aunt Chepa had passed away on December 25. The pharmacist apologetically told her, "I am terribly sorry for your loss, and it is very unfortunate that she lost her life. I remember a few weeks ago her husband continuously had been coming here to look for pain relief medication in order to sooth his wife's supposed migraines. I cannot imagine the headaches being anything other than migraines!" My mother thanked her for her concern and left the pharmacy with my grandmother's medication to share what she had learned.

In Nicaragua, it is very rare to find a mortuary, so the hospital helps wrap up the deceased in a white cloth and helps to lay her down in the back of the truck. My mother was disturbed from listening to the sound that her sister's body made when she fell on the floor of the truck. They started driving back home to La Concepcion, Masaya, Nicaragua, to prepare my aunt and the house for her funeral.

The house permeated with family, my aunt's church members, and my grandma's church members. The house was filled with love, sadness, prayers and songs. My cousin and her mom started dressing my aunt and putting make up on her, so she would not look as pale as she did. Meanwhile, the rest of my family started cooking for the guests. Everyone had a specific job during the funeral, and my grandmother was speaking to the crowd of devout Pentecostal Christians. She spoke with strong authority, while tears ran down her face. She fainted twice from a loss of energy and almost fell into the grave, trying to reach for her daughter.

During the service, and after my grandmother's eulogy, the guests, including my family and the preacher, had a continuous prayer that lasted quite a while. During that prayer, my mother had a very interesting experience after asking our Heavenly Father to show her that my aunt was fine. As she asked, she suddenly decided to open her eyes. When she did, she saw an apparition made entirely of light that took the form of my aunt who had a grand crown over her head and was accompanied by another apparition of a man who had his arm around her shoulder. He also had a very large crown over his head.

The Lord will not give us pain that we are unable to handle, and I believe truly that our God Himself decided this. My aunt died leaving behind no hate, grudge or sorrow. She created some beautiful memories with my mom and family.

During my grandma's visits, she would often fall asleep right before my aunt's aches began to occur. The majority of the time no one felt any traumatic experience from the loss of our family member, and thanks to our faith and our Lord that while most of us were depressed and some have slightly declined in health, we have been able to cope properly with the loss of a wonderful mother, aunt, and daughter. She had a beautiful and motherly heart, and I am proud to call her my aunt and my second mother.

Edited by Dr. C. White-Elliott

About the Author

    Jean Cedeno is a college student attending College of the Desert in order to achieve his career goal, which is to become a theoretical physicist. He is interested in a teaching profession in a university setting and is also interested in research opportunities. Jean Cedeno has had various volunteer opportunities as a tutor and a zooteen. He has fallen in love with the beauty of nature through science shows and documentaries.

A Mother's Heart IV

Ana Banana

Caroline Ferrer

Edited by Dr. C. White-Elliott

"I couldn't live without you love."

Petula Clark

A Mother's Heart IV

Dear Mom,

You were born Ana Marie Huerta on March 10, 1950, in Long Beach, California. Your parents were Jenaro and Alice Huerta. You had five siblings: Gloria, Ray, Linda, Lorraine, and Bobby. You became my mom on January 7, 1984. I am your third daughter.

I was expected to be a boy. I have always made comments in a humorous way, regarding my birth order. I would jokingly say that I was supposed to be a boy, not a girl, so mom and dad love my little brother more, as he was the son that was promised. Obviously, you understood they were jokes when my siblings and I would sit around the dinner table laughing with tears in our eyes.

Your ability to make light of dark situations was one of the many qualities I have admired and loved most about you, my beautiful mother. You were never an angry person nor hateful. You are the strongest person I know. The hardships we faced together through your divorce from my dad to the hardships of living in poverty. We were always surrounded with love and comfort from you.

We didn't have a lot of money, but our home was filled with laughter and love. You made sure we had a home. You took a shitty job bagging groceries at forty-two years old just because you knew we would eventually need braces. You gave up so much of your youth to provide for us. You continue to support and help each and every one of us whenever we call.

When you married our beloved stepdad Ernie, our lives were forever changed for the better. We have had stability and support from both of you. Our children have wonderful amazing grandparents. We can never tell you enough how much we love you both. My memories of you from childhood to adulthood warm my heart.

I can recall a time when I woke up from another night terror. I was no more than eight years old. I woke up at 3 am, looking for you next to me. I felt safest sleeping in your bed, so when you weren't there, I panicked slightly. I frantically paced from your room to the kitchen table, and there you were. Sitting down, clipping coupons with headphones on listening to Petula Clark's *Downtown*. You saw me standing there with my sweat-soaked pajamas and tears in my eyes.

In that moment, I needed my mommy. You took your headphones off and called me over to you with a smile on your face. I ran to you and snuggled onto your lap. You wiped my tears away and just held me knowing I needed one of your magic hugs to ease the anxiety of the nightmare. You then placed the headphones over my ears and let Petula's soft, sweet voice calm my fears and help me fall back to sleep. Even now, years later, I still play Petula Clark's *Downtown*, think of you, and smile with happy tears in my eyes.

You have always shielded us from sadness and had a way to make us forget our hurt. Your laugh is contagious and brings joy to our hearts. I know I can always call you anytime of the day and you will listen to me, whether I'm crying or simply want to hear your voice. I love you more than you can ever understand, and I will be forever grateful to you for my life.

Love your daughter,
Carol

About the Author

Caroline Ferrer is a student at Crafton Hills College. She is majoring in psychology and plans to transfer to a Cal State. She plans to become a therapist for victims of domestic violence. She currently lives in Redlands with her husband, Ignacio, and two children.

Edited by Dr. C. White-Elliott

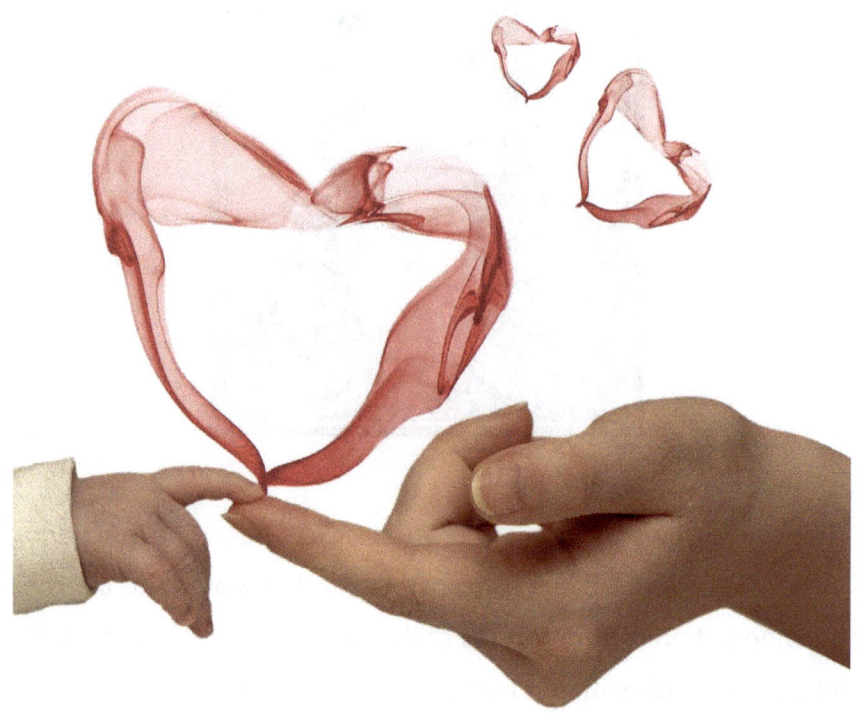

A Mother's Heart IV

Cherishing You

Joshua Garza

Edited by Dr. C. White-Elliott

"For I know the plans I have for you," declares the LORD,

"plans to **prosper you** *and not to harm you, plans*

to give you **hope** *and a* **future.** *"*

Jeremiah 29:11 (NIV)

A Mother's Heart IV

Dear Mom,

Happy Mother's Day. This is the day that represents who you are. The person you are in my eyes is an independent, unique, and loving woman. I know this may sound cliché, but I genuinely appreciate everything you have done and continue to do for me every day. Whether it is big or small, I will always take notice of all the hard work you have put into raising the man I am today. I have acknowledged all the trials and struggles you have been through to prosper and get you to where you are today. You deserve every ounce of happiness and what life still has to offer you.

Your independence is what I admire the most about you. Not only did you take on the role of a mother, but also the role of a father. You have been there for me and taking on both roles since long before I can remember. Since my early childhood years, I have watched you prove to yourself that you did not need another person to raise your child. I have seen the hustle and what you went through to get where you are financially and mentally today.

As I watched you raise me, I saw you strengthen yourself. You have always been an individual that did not need help from a man, and you would always tell yourself that you would not ever depend on one no matter how hard life would get. Through your years of prospering, when I was young, you always maintained a roof that I could lay my head under and not worry about anything because I knew I had a mother like you to protect me while I rested. As I grew older, the roofs where I lay my head may have changed and the places I grew up may have been in different locations, but you are the person that would make it feel like home.

Along with the houses changing, so did your cars, and wow, you have been through so many cars. I remember when we would have to drive with the windows rolled all the way down because the air conditioning did not work or when we would have to put water in the radiator because it would overheat. We can finally say now that going through all of those struggles led to your success of where you are now. I remember when you were finally able to go buy a brand new car right off the lot and we got rid of the Malibu because of the problems it contained. You had said, "Now, I will no longer have to stress about it breaking down somewhere."

I also recall the moment when you said we are moving to a better place like it was yesterday. While I was at school that day, you were out looking at new apartments. When I arrived home from school, you and I had went to look at our new and permanent home.

What makes you different from other mothers is your uniqueness. When I was young, you had the most unique style. You would wear sandals that had a net in the front that covered your toes with butterflies and flowers on them. There was only one store near our house that carried them, and you would buy them every time a new color came out. To go with your sandals, you would have a tank top to match. You would always have a brand new pair of white pants and shorts for special occasions because you would not want to get them dirty. Now that I am older, you come to me for advice on how to dress to keep up with the new generation.

Along with your choice of clothing, the way you would decorate was unique as well. I remember, in one of our apartments, you had a rooster phase. The kitchen had nothing but roosters from wall to wall. The tablecloth and table mats had roosters on them. The curtains and dish towels had roosters on them, too. After the rooster phase, you went through your palm tree phase. Palm trees have always been your favorite tree, and back then, you decided to incorporate it into our home. It went from roosters to palm trees. That phase was worse than the rooster phase. The entire house was decorated with them. You also bought pillows and area rugs with palm trees on them. The kitchen had palm tree themed tablecloths and placemats as well.

I remember our guests would come over and say how nice you had decorated, and I would hope they were joking. The phase you are affected by now is the color brown. When moving into the home we are in now, you had wanted to go with brown as the theme. Knowing that I enjoy decorating, you let me decorate the new apartment and because I love you so dearly, I even incorporated brown into the layout. Although you had gone through these phases and I tended to find them peculiar growing up, I grew to love them because they represent you now every time I see them.

Aside from many things changing in my childhood and through the process of raising me, your love has always remained the same. Your love is my stability, and it is the fuel that keeps me going to achieve my goals because I know I will always have your support. You have stood by me with every decision I make involving school, work and life in general. You accepted my preferences and gave me advice about what to look for in a person. You helped me get through my trials these last few years, and I could not have thanked you enough. I know that everything you have done for me was out of love.

Growing up, I used to hate when you would cry during my accomplishments because I thought you were just too sentimental and were ruining the moment. As I write this to you, I shed tears which is hypocritical of me, but I hope you do the same when reading it because your tears have a meaning behind them, and they are a meaning of love. You do not cry because you are sad, but you cry out of love. Although we are not perfect and share differences at times, you have shown me that no matter the situation, you will always have my back.

The day I confided in you, I was scared because I thought you were not going to accept my decision that I chose to take in life. I had negative thoughts that you were not going to support me and I was going to be left to deal with it on my own, but instead you stood by my side since then and supported my every action. Although we are not perfect and share our differences here and there, I will always love you unconditionally, and you have shown me you will do the same.

Once again, I cannot say it enough, but I love you for being the beautiful, independent, unique, and loving mother you have always been from the start. Even though I am now occupied with my life and we do not spend as much quality time as we used to, I will always cherish every moment we spend together whether it is for a short or long time. You deserve happiness and many blessings. Keep on knowing your worth and pushing forward. You are at a good place in time right now, and I cannot even imagine how much more you are going to accomplish from here on forth.
Love, your son.

About The Author

Joshua Garza was nineteen years of age at the time he created this work. Garza was born and raised in San Bernardino. He hopes to achieve his dream of earning a degree in nursing and apply his skills to helping the many who are in need of physical and mental care. He always brings out the good in people and is known for his positive energy that he radiates towards others. He aspires to be a role model to his nephew, nieces, and future children. He values every moment spent with his family and friends. He enjoys driving along the coasts of California and taking road trips through the deserts to admire their beauty and peaceful atmospheres.

Edited by Dr. C. White-Elliott

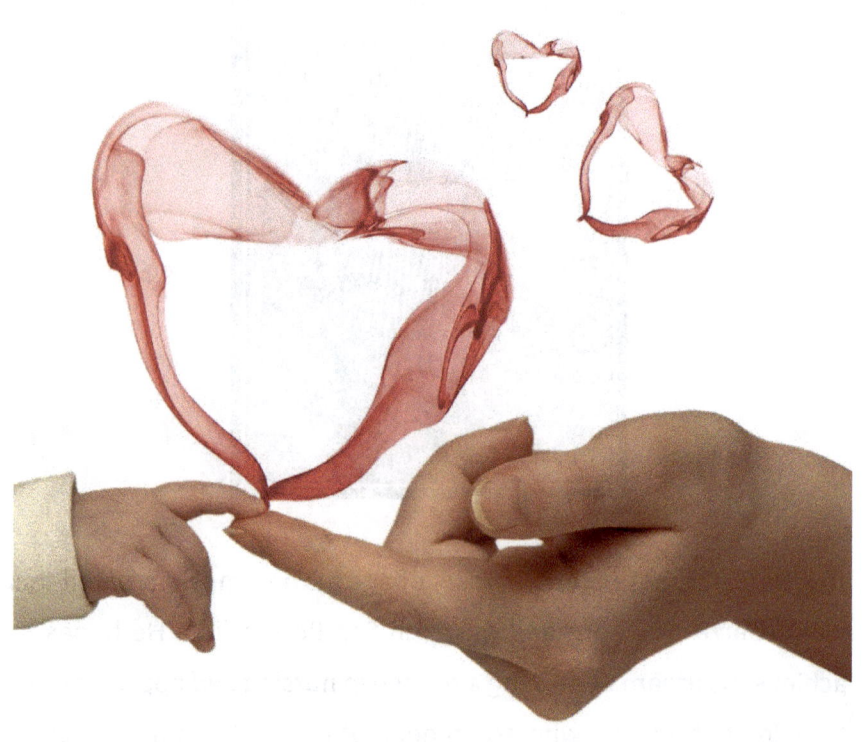

A Mother's Heart IV

To A Special Woman

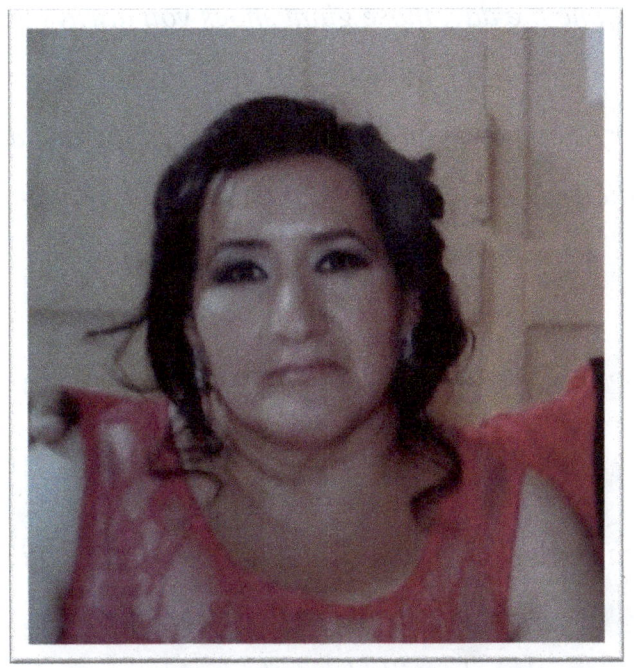

Yesenia Hernandez

Edited by Dr. C. White-Elliott

And then came the day, you are talking like her, you cook like her, sing like her, dance like her, cry like her.
Then came the day, those giant shoes you always tried on, now they fit you.
In every step now, you understand everything one day you criticized. You understand the limits, the challenges, angriness, the fears, the concepts.
And you are thankful that she was there, always close, taking care of you.
You are thankful of those sleepless nights, sacrifices and the time.
Then came the day, you look at the mirror, and you see her.
For months you were inside her, but she will always be inside you.

Unknown Author

A Mother's Heart IV

Time flies fast, and sometimes, I do not take the time to appreciate and thank the person who is there for me. Sometimes, it's work, school, or other activities. Time is always an issue, running from one place to another, but today is the day to recognize a wonderful woman.

You started very young being a mom, giving up on your dreams and your goals. You spent sleepless night taking care of me, because of a flu, watching for my fever. Sometimes, I'd wake you up just because I was scared of monsters, and I could not sleep. You were there for me.

I remember when I was a kid, you were always so busy taking us to school, cooking, cleaning, shopping, and making sure we were on time, and I wondered how you managed your time with all those activities, while having four children of different ages, without the physical support of my dad. I do not remember you crying or complaining about your situation. I just remember you being happy.

We were in Mexico, and Dad was so far from us, but you had the courage to not let all that destroy you or make you weak. You are a strong woman. Maybe, inside, you were afraid, not knowing what to do, but you never showed it.

As I grew up, many things changed, such as moving to California to be with Dad. You started working, and not seeing you after school and spending time together was one of the things I missed the most. You are always supporting everyone, sacrificing your happiness to make us happy, and I always wondered why. You always placed yourself second. There were times I judged you for always putting someone else first, instead of yourself, and when you got mad at me and tried to give me advice, and I did not want to listen.

At that time, I did not understand you or your position as a mother. Time has changed now, and I am in your position as a mother, and I have begun to understand you more. Now, I know why you always put yourself second because you love me and you want the best for me. I understand all the sacrifices you made because now I am doing it for my daughter. Now, I understand your worries, your anger, your dedication, and your advice. Now, I understand that you became strong for us and the unconditional love you have for us.

At times, I did not appreciate all you had done for me, such as the night you stayed with me at the hospital when my daughter was born, taking care of both of us. Thanks for helping me take care of my daughter. Now, I understand you more. When I think back on all the times I took you for granted when I was younger, never once did you give up on me. No matter how many times I hurt you or broke your heart, you were always waiting for me with a smile and a hug.

Now, I am in your shoes and to be honest, it's not easy. There are times I want to give up, but I remember you never gave up. Now, I know how you felt when Dad was not there to help you or when you had no one to count on. I am in your shoes, but I still cannot fit them yet. There is more I have to learn, but I know you will be there for me. I admire you even more for being the best, strongest, loving mom that you are.

Time keeps flying, and I do not want to waste more time without saying that I love you and I am thankful to God for giving

A Mother's Heart IV

me the best mom. I am taking the time to recognize and appreciate everything you do. Now is the time to thank you for all you have done for me, supporting me even when I have let you down. I am not a perfect daughter, but for me, you are the perfect mom and grandmother. I want to thank you for your support, your advice, your dedication, your patience, and your love. I also want to apologize for the times I let you down. I know you always want the best for me, and you worked hard to give me the best you time. You are the most important woman in my life. Thank you, Mom, for all you have done and shown me. Thank you for encouraging me to never give up on my dreams and for believing in me when no one did. Thanks to you, I became the woman and the mother that I am.

There are no words that can describe what you mean to me and how important you are in my life. You are always giving without asking for anything in return, but today, I want to recognize your effort, your dedication, your love for me and to tell you that I feel fortunate to have you as my mom. I love you, Mom.

Muchas gracias por todo lo que me has dado y ensenado no tengo palabras para agradecerte. Talvez, no te lo digo todo el tiempo pero eres la persona mas importante en mi vida y te quiero mucho. Gracias por cuidar de mi y de mi hija, estar cuando mas te necesito, apoyarme, y creer en mi. Eres una mujer fuerte, amorosa, siempre das sin pedir nada a cambio. Te pido perdon por lastimarte y decepcionarte tantas veces, cuando tu solo me as demostrado tu amor. No soy perfecta y se que seguire cometiendo errores, pero se que estaras ahi para guiarme y apoyarme. Me siento tan afortunada de que tu seas mi mama, una maravillosa mujer que da todo por su famila. Te admiro por ser una exelente, mujer, esposa, amiga, pero sobre todo por ser la mejor mama. Ahora que soy madre te comprendo mas, tus angustias, tus enojos, pero ahora entiendo mas tus consejos, aquellos que alguna vez no quize escuchar. Ahora soy yo la que esta en tus zapatos, solo espero tenerte cerca para que me guies. Debo confesarte que no es facil ser madre, ahora te entiendo mas y agradesco todo lo que hiciste por mi. Gracias por todo, te Quiero Mama.

Con Amor,
Tu hija

About the Author

Yesenia Hernandez was born in Mexico. She is currently a resident of California. She is a young woman with dreams and goals to achieve. She loves the beach, the sunset, to travel, and to help others. She is a single mother of a six-year-old daughter whom she loves and is her motivation to be successful in life. Yesenia is a dedicated, responsible, positive, outgoing person, and the first of her family to enter college.

Edited by Dr. C. White-Elliott

A Dedication to the Strongest Woman

Casey Howard

Edited by Dr. C. White-Elliott

"I'm selfish, impatient, and a little insecure. I make mistakes, I am out of control, and at times, hard to handle. But if you can't handle me at my worst, then you sure as hell don't deserve me at my best."

Marilyn Monroe

A Mother's Heart IV

This woman has a heart of gold and is headstrong. She loves sweets and can't resist a diet Coke when it's available. She is a binge watcher of Netflix and has gotten to a point where she has begun to watch Spanish soap operas just to pass the time. But with all these dorky qualities to her personality, she is by far the best person in my life right now. She is my real life superhero, and her name is Samantha Ann Howard.

For as long as I can remember, my mom has told me she always wanted kids. She said she wanted her someday husband to work while she devoted her time and life to her beautiful children. So, when she met her soon-to-be husband in a local bar, she got her wish, but she didn't realize it yet. She wanted kids, but still to this day, she says she was shocked when she found out she was pregnant with my older sister Brittany. I still don't know if it was a happy shock that she finally got her wish or if the reality sank in that my dad was the father of her daughter. My mom and dad weren't dating very long when they got pregnant, but they still decided to get married.

Through the years, all was going well, so my mom and dad decided to plan for five years later and have little old me. My sister hated that I wasn't a boy. She had said she wanted a baby brother. Then by accident again, my mom got pregnant with my baby brother Steven. Seriousness aside, I was the only one planned. Just saying. Even though my mom didn't expect to have three kids, she still loved us with all her heart. But, I don't think she expected to have three wild and crazy kids.

Growing up, my siblings and I always fought. When I was younger, I would twist my brother's ears until they turned red. Also,

I would try to take my clothes off every chance I got. My siblings did as much as I did, but the list of their troubles is a mile long. As we grew older, we would punch and scream, while yelling how much we hated each other. We were very violent children. And, of course, we know all these stories because my mom always waits for the right situations to embarrass my siblings and me. Because of these stories, my siblings and I can now laugh at the past. We are now closer than ever, and my siblings, Brittany and Steven, and I are adults and our affection is what it is because of our mom.

For as long as I can remember, we moved a lot. Sometimes, we would stay in the same area, but move to a different house. Moving was a common thing for my family. I think even back then, my mom dreaded moving, but she never showed her feelings to my siblings and me. She never liked showing us she was upset. So, she made moving fun. When we knew we were moving, she would let us have an opinion on what we thought of the house. She would let us tag along and let us debate who would get which room.

Now, some of you are thinking, "Where is the dad?" My mom used to describe his personality as a 'workaholic.' He was never home. He would leave very early and come home around dinner time. My mom was the best thing for my siblings and me while we were growing up. She was so strong for taking on both roles. She stayed up late helping with math, God bless her soul, and making sure we were cared for, while giving us the best childhood. My mom never let my dad not being around faze her into not doing the best she could do. But, I don't think she expected him to divorce her in the worst possible way.

A Mother's Heart IV

It was Christmas Eve. My dad told my mom on Christmas Eve that he didn't want to be married to my sweet loving mother anymore. I'm still pissed that my dad could be so heartless. I never did get to ask her why she didn't raise hell. I would have thrown him out of the house or made him sleep in the car or on the couch. Now that I'm twenty-one, I still don't get it. My mom was strong after that day. She didn't grovel at her loss; she got her ass in gear and took care of her responsibilities.

I think that is what I love most about my mom. She never lost focus on what she wanted for my siblings and me in life. She did what she knew was best for us. She kept us in Lake Elsinore, California because she knew that was where our life was, and she allowed us to finish high school there. She even got a second job just so we could get everything we needed or wanted. I could never thank her enough for that. Even as a grown woman, I don't think I could be brave enough to raise three kids on my own.

My mom was finally set free and became the best person she could become after her divorce from my dad. She is much happier, and it shows. She laughs more and is never afraid to voice her opinion. *At all.* She loves her job as a teacher's aide at a cute little elementary school. The kids she works with keeps her on her toes, but I think she secretly loves it, at least from the way she re-tells her day every night at dinner.

I'm also proud that she is sticking by her dreams and going back to school. My mom always wanted to be teacher, and I know she will be the best damn teacher there will ever be.

When I was coming of age from a girl to a woman, I strove to be like her when I grew up. I wanted to be brave like her and handle the hard shit -head on- even if it scared the crap out of me. I want to follow my dreams like her and maybe become a teacher. I want to do something with English, but she says teacher all the way. So maybe. I want to be feisty like her and not take shit from anyone. But, I think I got that one covered already. When I was a young girl, my mom used to call me her little mini-me. At the time, I didn't believe her, but now that I am a grown woman, I believe her. I may be a little bit too much like her.

Even though I am living on my own, I still thrive to be like her. She taught me to be the woman I am today, so I want to make her proud. Everything I do is for her. She is who I don't want to disappoint.

A Letter to My Greatest Hero

Mom, I love you with all my heart. I can't thank you enough for everything you have done for me as well as Brittany and Steven. We are forever thankful for you being our mom. I wouldn't be here writing in a book, dedicating a story of my love for you, if it wasn't for you. I strive to be like you. You are a badass person for taking the role of mother and father and doing it like a pro. With Dad gone, you gave us enough love and support that him absence seemed less important because I knew you would never leave us behind. I want you to know that even if I don't live with you anymore, I still miss you every day. There are times that I am so homesick that I want to move back, but your weekly phone calls help a lot. Just hearing your voice soothes me.

Thank you for always believing in me when I thought no one else would. Thank you for being kind and sweet. Thank you for making us laugh by bringing up stories of our childhood and on occasion wrestling Steven to floor when he thinks you can't. You are my best friend, my supporter, and the greatest mom on the planet. There are so many other things I am thankful for, but the most important one is **I Thank You For Being You!**

I Love You, Mom!

Edited by Dr. C. White-Elliott

About the Author

Casey Lynn Howard was born on September 30, 1997, in Las Vegas, Nevada. She has two siblings: Brittany Howard, who is her older sister, and Steven Howard, who is her little brother. Then, there is Brandon Young (her older brother), whom she found less than two years ago. Casey's favorite hobby by far is to read romance novels. She has read over 200 books and has no plan to stop any time soon. She is a sophomore in college, and she is an English major, hoping to be surrounded by books in the long future ahead.

A Mother with Super Powers

Jordan Rice

Edited by Dr. C. White-Elliott

A Mother's Heart IV

The word "mother" is just a term to some. And, some mothers do not realize what it takes to actually be one. So, what does it mean to be a mother? I've seen them all- from the valued to the despised- not only by their peers but by their own children due to their neglect of participation in motherly duties.

Lana Johnson, mother of six, did everything a mother could possibly due to complete her motherly duties for each and every single one of her children, nieces, and nephews. I, Jordan Rice, her fourth born and second son, have personally witnessed the superpowers she possesses as a mother, but I could not have witnessed it all. With the help of a few memories from my siblings (Breanna Fant, Marlena Johnson, and Nicole Hayse) I have put together a series of stories to honor our dear mother on this beautiful Mother's Day. For, we have all witnessed the stress and sacrifices our mother endured just to make sure her babies were well taken care of.

To begin, Lana Johnson was born on November 29, 1971. She had her first born, Nicole, at age sixteen in 1988. Then, following in 1990, came along Christian and Chrishun. Unfortunately, Chrishun didn't make it long in the world and sadly passed away at a few months old. Marlena was then born in 1992. Then, I. Jordan, was born in 1994. Then, the youngest two, Brian in 1997 and Breanna in 1999, were added to the crew. So, as you can see, we were all born very close in age. And, mom made sure we stuck together while growing up, never forgetting we were all we had.

Mom sacrificed a lot of time with us because she was a single parent and needed to keep a roof over our head and food in our bellies. I still sometimes even as an adult fail to understand how she did it. Her superpowers were at work to somehow make things come together. At times, we (even as kids) knew things weren't going right, but she would tell us, "Everything is going to be alright," and it always was. My mom worked as a pharmacy technician, so she did not earn a lot of money, but she did provide enough. And, each and every one of us will tell you to this day that we appreciate her without hesitation.

Throughout our adolescence, hardships came and went. One hardship we faced was having our electricity cut off. When those instances occurred, normally, my mom would take us out and about, and by the time we came back, the lights would be back on. Well, one day in 2005 or 2006, we were at the library all day, and on our way back home, I saw a pizza parlor and wanted pizza. I remember the pizza parlor was near the campus of Akron University, and the sign on the window said, "Buy One, Get Two Free." Mom immediately said, "No," but when I told her about the deal, she decided maybe it would be a good idea.

When we arrived home, after walking for miles because we could not afford a car, the power was cut off. We blindly gathered in my mom's room on the floor next to her bed to eat. I could hear my mom sniffling as though she was crying, but I could not see, so I asked if she was okay. Of course, she responded that she was fine, telling me to just eat. My heart sank so deep into my stomach that I did not want to eat anymore; I just wanted my mom to be happy.

There were many hard times we all went through together, and I believe it is what makes us so close now. We, as siblings, look after one another and make sure we're all doing well. That comes from the bond of hurting together and prospering together.

I have friends who would probably still to this day never know what it is to go without or to have their parents miss a meal because there was just enough food for their children. I wouldn't wish that struggle on anybody. One thing my mom proved to us and helped us prove to ourselves is that if only the strong survives, then we must be hulks because we crawled out the depths of hell, resurfaced ourselves, and know that we could do it again.

Here is an account shared by my sister Nicole about how she was a witness to some of our mom's superpowers.

I've always admired my mother for her strength. She has taken on the world, and she has been through so many trials and tribulations that were designed to make the average person break down and crack. However, my mother always held her head up high, put on her supermom cape, and managed to overcome every situation that was thrown her way, without ever losing faith. However, if she did, my siblings and I never knew of it.

Raising five children, basically on her own, was a hard task by itself. My siblings and I didn't make things easy for her either. We fought like normal kids, but there were five of us, and my mom did the best she could while diffusing the many sibling rivalries. She always made sure we knew how important it was for us to stick together. She instilled great values and morals within all of her children. It wasn't easy raising us on her own, while dealing with the extensive unnecessary issues our fathers gave her.

There were times when I could see that my mom was at her breaking point with all the things she was dealing with. Being the oldest of her children, I saw and understood what my younger siblings did not, but she never once showed them that she was at her breaking point, stressed, or fed up. She never missed a beat with "I love you's," hugs, and kisses, even when she was broken down.

One particular event that will forever be embedded in my memory and really made me see how strong my mother was/is was my grandmother's funeral. I was amazed at how my mother was able to not only organize and make the arrangements with very little to no help from her siblings. In the hardest, heartbreaking moment of her life, my mother completely took over the services and made sure her mother's homegoing services were exactly what my granny would have wanted.

My mother pulled herself together, with her voice cracking, her heart broken, and her eyes full of tears, in front of family and friends, and read three or four beautiful poems she had written. No one else could get up and say anything because it was too hard to get any words out, not my uncle or aunty or my pawpaw. But, my mother, as she has done so many times in her life, put on her supermom cape, and in the time when she understandably should have broken down, she found her strength and pushed through the very moment we all fear facing one day.

I always tell her I don't know how she could do it and how she made it through any of the situations she dealt with. Her reply has been the same ever since I can remember: "It's the love that I have for you, your siblings, and my granny babies that keeps me going.

If it wasn't for you guys, I would have no reason to keep going. My fear is you guys feeling the pain of losing me, so I will do all I can while I'm here to show you guys how much I love you."

Next, Marlena shares her memories.

The memories I have of my mother are just small pieces of a puzzle that is Lana Marie, a woman who endured countless ordeals to care for my siblings and me. Growing up, I couldn't comprehend the pain she was living in or the sacrifices she made to give us the best upbringing she could. Only now is she slowly revealing small truths of our complex past and all she went through to raise us. It is now, more than ever, I can say without a shadow of doubt that I am proud to call her "Mom."

I remember her coming home late at night from the hospital in powder blue and royal blue printed scrubs. She sat down on the couch exhausted, with her wild curls framing her face. In the orange glow of our living room, I knew for a fact she was an angel. I sat down on the floor and began massaging her feet as she told me about her day. I couldn't understand what she was saying, but as she went on, I thought to myself that I needed to be there. I needed to be the one to make sure she was okay at the end of the day- at the end of every day.

I remember the tears she shed the first time she saw us after we had been taken into state custody. She kissed us all and told us everything would be alright. Nearly a year later, she won us back.

I remember my dad pulling her up the stairs by her hair. Her foot was in a boot, and her crutches were sliding down the steps.

She told me she was okay and to go play. She said I didn't need to be worried because he wasn't hurting her.

I remember her cleaning up bits of muffins off the kitchen floor, still in scrubs from work earlier. My siblings, friends and I had a food fight in the kitchen. We crumbled the pastries my mom had baked in our hands and tossed them in all directions. She didn't get mad; instead, she told me it is good for kids to have fun, that it was okay, and I didn't have to worry.

All throughout my life, my mother kept a positive demeanor. It was her mask, her shield, her sword. When she was homeless, when she was tired, when her heart was broken, and when her mother died, my mother did her best to find the silver lining and wear it like a life vest.

No matter the situation, she promised us it was going to be okay, that we were going to get through it and to hold our heads up and keep on keeping on. I may not have inherited her positive outlook on life, but her words find me in the darkest of times.

When I feel the world caving in, when my anxiety is wringing me dry, when I can't see the light, I can hear her words. "Everything is going to be alright, Nina; don't worry." Sometimes, it's her voice that brings me back from the edge, and sometimes, it's her words that come out when I am comforting another person. I feel so lucky to have learned from this woman, and I'm so honored to call her Mom.

Last, but not least, Breanna shares her experience by expressing the time she broke her foot.

A Mother's Heart IV

It all started because my mother was talking (per usual- if you know her). I love my mother very much, with all my heart, as one would say, but this is one thing sticks with me. She just needed to turn, turn around and see what I had learned, my new tricks that I had practiced about two hours prior to her arrival.

It was a nice sunny weekend in March at my sister's grandma's house. My mom would drop me off to spend the weekend with her all the time; she was my best friend. We were not related by blood, but you know how that goes. She was my sister's grandmother. So, Friday came, and I packed my bag and got ready to go. My mom was waiting outside for me. We got there, said our "I love you's," and I went into the house. My sister and I always made potatoes together. I'm not sure why. We just did. We ate dinner, watched movies, and went to bed.

Saturday morning came, and my sister and I went exploring. I'm from Akron where forests are everywhere, and my brothers and I explored almost every day. When I moved to the desert, there were no forests to roam, so I had to make do with the small patches of trees here and there with the dried brown grass. So, behind my sister's house, there was one of those dry patches. It was a pretty good size; on the other side was a golf course. We would walk across the street to the park and hang out there for a while and go back home when it was too hot for us to stay out any longer. We watched tv and hung out for the rest of the night. Little did I know, the next day I wouldn't be able to walk.

On Sunday morning, my cousins came over. The neighbors had a trampoline that we would jump on, and we had planned to do that on that day. We jumped for hours, practicing flips and all types of tricks. I had perfected my flip. (At least, I thought I did). My mom was coming, so I packed my stuff and went back out to jump my heart out before I had to return home.

My mom came while my cousin and I were jumping, and she started talking (per usual). I thought I should show her a couple of flips, so I practiced a few, and then I called her to show her. I started jumping and getting higher. Then, I executed a perfect front flip, and I looked over. She was freaking talking and not paying attention. So, I yelled her name again, to make sure she was paying attention. I started jumping, getting my height up. My cousin was slightly bouncing too (mistake number one because it messed up the rhythm of my jumping). So, I prepared for my flip, and I flipped. When I came down, the bounce of the trampoline was coming up, so my ankle collided with it. I heard the snaps. There were two; my ankle was broken. I yelled for my mom. She thought my ankle was sprained. It was not.

We got ready to go to the hospital, but the car wouldn't start (just my luck). I was still in pain on the trampoline. My sister and my mom were standing by the edge of the trampoline. My cousin was still in the corner, and the car still hadn't started. An ambulance was called, but the wait seemed like forever. When it got there, the paramedics had to pull me off the trampoline. There was a net around it, so I only had one way out. They placed me on a stretcher and put a big orange inflatable brace around my ankle. Then, we got into the ambulance. It was the worst ride of my life. It was very bumpy, and with every bump, more pain came.

Finally, we arrived to the hospital. I got into a wheelchair, and I was wheeled into the waiting room with my giant orange inflatable

A Mother's Heart IV

brace. It was the longest wait of my life. Someone even bumped into to me like they didn't even notice my giant orange inflatable. When I finally went to the back, x-rays were done, and they hurt more than the break. The technician twisted my ankle to get all the right angles. I was taken to my bed and given pain meds.

I remember sitting there with my mom. I was so scared, but she told me something that I live by to this day. Whenever I was scared, she would say, "Fear is a *false expectation appearing real*." She always knows what to say to make me not scared even when she's not with me. I often think back on her words. First, my mom talks too much sometimes, and second is that little saying that will always stay with me.

ABOUT THE AUTHOR

Jordan attends College of the Desert.

A Mother's Heart IV

Gracias Mamá

Christopher Rodriguez

Edited by Dr. C. White-Elliott

I can always depend on my mama
And when it seems that I'm hopeless
You say the words that can get me back in focus
When I was sick as a little kid
To keep me happy there's no limit to the things you did
And all my childhood memories
Are full of all the sweet things you did for me
And even though I act crazy
I gotta thank the Lord that you made me
There are no words that can express how I feel
You never kept a secret, always stayed real
And I appreciate, how you raised me
And all the extra love that you gave me
I wish I could take the pain away
If you can make it through the night there's a brighter day
Everything will be alright if ya hold on
It's a struggle every day, gotta roll on
And there's no way I can pay you back
But my plan is to show you that I understand
You are appreciated

Tupac Amaru Shakur

A Mother's Heart IV

I do not know how to start this off. I suppose the best way to start this off is by saying, "Thank you." Thank you to all the mothers out there for loving their children. Thank you, Mom, for making me into the young man I am today. Thank you for everything you have done for me; I truly do not know what I would have done without you. You have been there for me for every aspect of my life, whether it be school or personal problems, such as friends and relationships. Thank you, Mom, for being my mom. However, I'm getting a little bit ahead of myself. I would like to share who my mom is.

My mother's name is Maria; she was born and raised in Mexico. She has a huge family, about eleven siblings in total. She was somewhere in the middle; our family is so huge that I never had the chance to meet some of them. My mother met my dad, Carlos, in Mexico, during high school. They were high school sweethearts, if you will, and they have been together ever since. It was pretty rough down in Mexico during their time, a lot of gangs, violence, and not a lot of opportunities to make something of oneself.

After they graduated high school, my dad and his family (my aunt and grandmother) wanted to move to America to have a new life. My dad asked my mom to go with him to start fresh, have a family of their own, and to make something of themselves. My mom did not know what to think of the difficult decision. She did have some family in America, but she hardly knew them, and she did not know any English. However, what she did know was that she was in love with my dad, and she knew she wanted a better life for her kids than the one she had.

So, she went with my dad and his family to America. Of course, she was down-hearted, leaving everything behind: her friends, her family, and her life. However, she also had a sense of excitement and hope because she was going to the land of opportunities with the one she loved to start a new life. She knew it would be the most difficult thing she would ever do, but she was ready to overcome any obstacles to make sure she received the life she had always wanted.

I am so proud of my mom; she is such a strong woman. To have the courage to move to a new country and start a new life is something I think most people would not do. It's a good thing my mom is not like most people.

When my mother and father first arrived in America, they lived with my father's mother, and after sometime, my dad and mom decided to move out. They moved into a house located in San Bernardino, and that's when my mom had my older brother, Ryan. My dad was working one job as a janitor, and my mom would sometimes help him with cleaning. My mom could not get an official job yet because she did not have her papers. So, she would have other small jobs to help make money, such as babysitting. Then, my grandmother moved in with my parents after about a year. My grandmother would take care of Ryan while my mother worked. When my mother returned home, she would look after my brother and take care of the house.

Unfortunately, after five years, what my parents earned was not sufficient, so they had to move out of their home. They moved into an apartment in Rialto and continued on with life. It had to get worse before it could get better, and it did. They were living comfortably there for a while. It was a nice little place, and my father had a stable job to provide for the family. Then, my mother became pregnant with me, Chris, who turned out to be the heaviest of her three children at birth. When I was born, I weighed approximately ten pounds. "Again, sorry, Mom."

The apartment was not large enough for two children and three adults, so we had to move one more time. My parents purchased a two-story house in Highland. However, the more things they obtained, the more they had to sacrifice. My dad and mom had to work a lot more often while my grandmother from my mom's side of the family took care of the house, Ryan, and me. For now, let us call her abuela because that is how I remember her.

Unfortunately, my grandma from my dad's side had passed away. Things were a bit rough, but my mother was taking care of her responsibilities and had an excellent balance with home and work. A year later, she became pregnant with the last of the family: Noemi, my little sister. My mom was so excited and happy to be having a little girl. Soon, the family consisted of my dad, my mom, Ryan, me, and Noemi. But, that was when things became a lot harder for my mom. My dad picked up two full-time jobs, and my mom would help him with his janitorial job, while taking care of the family. I remember her taking care of the family from morning to evening.

At night, she would leave with my dad to help him with his janitorial jobs. They wouldn't come back until midnight; other times, they would not return until one in the morning. While my parents were away, my grandma would take care of us. I would only see my dad for a short period of time when he came to pick up my mom or on the weekends. Other than that, my dad was mostly gone, working to provide for the family. My mom was working a part-time job (with my father at night), taking care of the house, and taking care of three kids. Now that is a mom who is dedicated to her family. And I still thank her to this day for it.

In 2005, I was five years old; my little sister was three years old; my brother was starting high school; and, my parents were still working. While my parents went to work, instead of my grandma watching us, it was Ryan. My abuela could not watch over us because she became ill. As a kid, I absolutely loved my abuela; she would always take care of us. I also remembered how much she meant to my mom.

One day, I was playing with my little sister in our room, and we got hungry. We walked down the hall to find our mom, so she could make us something to eat. At the time, I was still five, so I did not know a lot, but I knew enough. I could see my mom on the phone with a look of worry and concern. I tried to get her attention, but she calmly told me, "Please, mijo. Give me one minute, and I will make you something." She continued to talk on the phone, but I did not know who it was.

I asked her, "Who is that, Mamá?"

She replied, with a crack in her voice, "It is the doctor, mijo." I did not understand why she was talking to the doctor, so I kept asking questions.

"Why are you talking to the doctor?" I asked with curiosity.

She looked at me with eyes full of stress and said, "It is about your grandma." I still could not tell what was wrong. However, I could tell my mom was overwhelmed with sadness.

A Mother's Heart IV

I simply stood there holding my little sister's hand, not saying a word, while waiting for our mom. She finally hung up the phone and sunk her face into her forearm, while bending over her desk. That was the first time I had ever seen my mother cry.

I asked her, "What's wrong, Mamá?"

It took her two minutes to reply and say, "Grandma's gone, mijo." I looked at her puzzled because I still did not understand what was happening at the time.

I asked her, "Where did she go?"

She told me with tears running down her face, "She left, mijo."

"Will she be back?" I asked.

My mom put her hand on each of our shoulders, looked at us and said, "She can't come back."

After that line, she looked away and started tearing again. I did not know what that meant, but what I did know was that I had to comfort our mom. I pulled my sister with me as I walked to her leg.

I looked at her and said, "But you still have us, Mamá. We are never leaving." She looked back at us with teary eyes and a heartwarming feeling. She got down on her knees and gave us a hug and said in a soft-spoken voice, "I know, mijo. I know." I remember that day so vividly because to me that was the first day I felt I had done something for her, being there for my mom in one of her most difficult times in life and giving her comfort, letting her know I love her and that she will never be alone.

Mom, you are such an incredible and courageous woman. You went through so much, and I am so proud I am your son. I wish I could do more for you, but over time, I realized what you wanted for your kids. You wanted us to have a life better than the one you had. That is why everything I accomplished was for you, Mom. It was to show you that you did a phenomenal job at being a mother. There are so many things I am grateful for, Mom. I cannot fit them all into this short story. I know it was not much of a story, but I wanted to remind you of everything you have overcome and accomplished. Ryan has his own real estate business. I am the first in our family to go to college and win awards for my academics. And, Noemi is always out, wanting to help others and to become a teacher for special education children. Mom, you did such a good job, and I thank you for it. Thank you, Mom, for being the person I can always depend on. Thank you, Mom. I will always love you.

About The Author

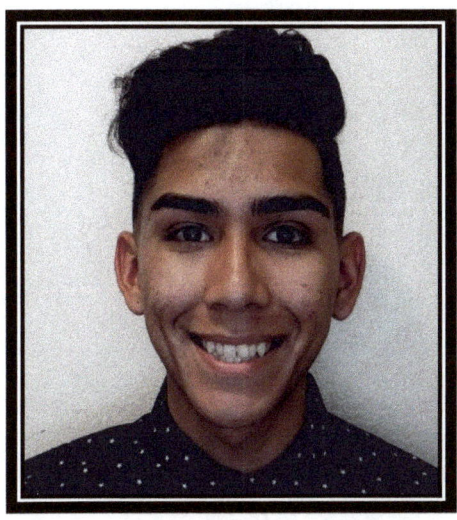

Christopher Rodriguez is an eighteen-year-old student attending Crafton Hills College and wants to transfer to a Cal State. His major is in technical theater, and he wants to become a set designer for theater shows. Chris enjoys spending time with his family, friends, and girlfriend. Chris was a part of the Blackhawk Theater at Citrus Valley and has won numerous awards and recognition. Chris also enjoys areas throughout the performing arts like acting, singing, and dancing.

Edited by Dr. C. White-Elliott

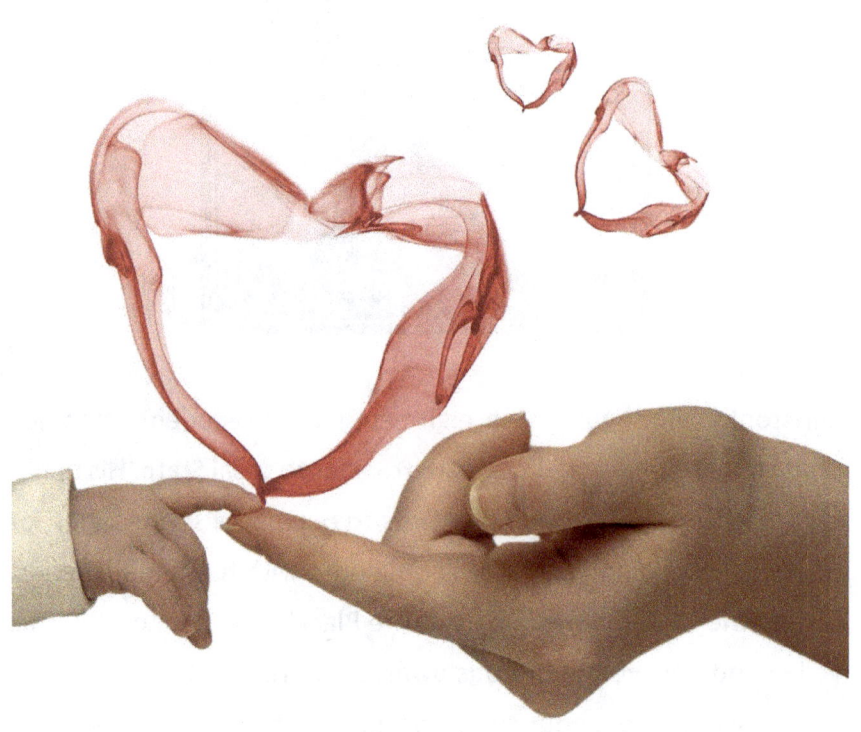

Gift of Salvation
for Non-Believers

"For all have sinned, and come short of the glory of God."

(Romans 3:23)

This section was written especially for non-believers, those who have not accepted the gift of salvation. The gift of salvation saves souls from eternal damnation and is a free gift offered by God Himself.

John 3:16-18 says, *"For God so loved the world, that he gave his only begotten Son, that whosoever believeth in him should not perish, but have everlasting life. For God sent not his Son into the world to condemn the world; but that the world through him might be saved. He that believeth on him is not condemned: but he that believeth not is condemned already, because he hath not believed in the name of the only begotten Son of God."*

This section of scripture tells us God's purpose for giving His son Jesus to the world. The world was in a bad condition. The world was overwrought with sin; the people were living for fleshly desires rather than for God's desires.

As a result of the world's conditions, God decided He would offer the perfect sacrifice that would save the world from being a place where people were lost and had no hope. He decided that His own son could stand in proxy for the sin-filled world, taking all sin upon Himself.

So, Jesus came, born of a virgin, to save this dying world. He walked on this earth for 33 ½ years, doing the work of His Heavenly Father. At the appointed time, He died by way of crucifixion upon a cross at Calvary, on Golgotha's hill. He shed His blood and died for you and for me. Because His blood was pure, it paid the penalty for all unrighteousness and gave those who believe in Him direct access to His father's throne.

Scripture tells us in Matthew 27:51 that the veil of the temple was ripped in two from top to bottom, at the moment that Jesus' spirit left His body. As a result of the veil's removal, we are no longer required to have a high priest make intercession for us. We, as the children of the Most High God, are able to approach the throne God for ourselves, and Jesus sits on the right hand of the Father making intercession for us.

But what is even more miraculous than God offering His own son as the perfect sacrifice was the fact that when Jesus was placed in grave clothes and placed in a tomb, He only remained there until the third day. God would not have it that His son would remain in the heart of the earth forever. In order for people to believe in the awesome power of God and His dear son Jesus, a miracle had to be performed. So, on the third day, after Jesus died on the cross, He was resurrected, demonstrating the omnipotence of God. This very act was the act that would cause people to believe in a god that reigns supreme and holds the power of the universe in His very hands, a god that could save them from themselves.

Today, if you are an unbeliever, you can change your destiny. You can change where you will spend your eternity. Our Heavenly Father gives us the freedom of choice about how we want to live our life here on earth and how we want to spend eternity. In Deuteronomy 30:19, God boldly declares, *"I call heaven and earth to record this day against you, that I have set before you life and death, blessing and cursing: therefore choose life, that both thou and thy seed may live."*

So, dear friend what choice will you make today? Will you spend your eternity with the Creator or will you suffer Hell's eternal flames? Again, the choice is yours. Just as the men aboard the ship who were with Jonah became believers, you too can make a choice to accept the only one and true living God as your god.

If after reading the above passages, you have decided that you want to spend your eternity in Heaven with God, the creator, and His son Jesus, and the Holy Spirit, read through what has affectionately come to be known as the Roman's Road. This is the road to salvation. As you read through the scriptures that comprise the Roman's Road, you will also read the explanation for each scripture so you will have clarity about what you are reading and confessing.

The Roman's Road to Salvation

The road to salvation begins with Romans 3:23 which declares, *"For all have sinned, and come short of the glory of God."* This scripture explains that everyone has come short of God's glory and needs redemption. Then Romans 6:23a states, *"For the wages of sin is death."* Here, we learn that the consequence of living a life of sin is death. Everyone will experience physical death as a result of the sin committed in the garden of Eden, but those who commit themselves to a life of sin will suffer eternal damnation in the lake of fire (Rev. 19).

Continue with the rest of verse 6:23 that says, *"but the gift of God is eternal life through Jesus Christ our Lord."* There is an alternative to suffering eternal damnation. We can accept the gift of salvation by accepting Jesus as our personal lord and savior. Then, Romans 5:8 says, *"But God commendeth his love toward us, in that, while we were yet sinners, Christ died for us."* We are able to receive the gift of salvation because Christ came to earth and shed His blood for us on the cross.

Continue to Romans 10: 9-10 which says, *"That if thou shalt confess with thy mouth the Lord Jesus, and shalt believe in thine heart that God hath raised him from the dead, thou shalt be saved. For with the heart man believeth unto righteousness; and with the mouth confession is made unto salvation."* If we confess with our mouths that Jesus is the son of God, that he came and died for our sins, and that God raised Him from the dead, we will receive salvation.

Finish with Romans 10:13, which states, *"For whosoever shall call upon the name of the Lord shall be saved."* Call upon the name of God by saying these words, "**Lord Jesus, come into my heart and save me Lord. I believe that you are the Son of God who came and died on the cross for my sins. I believe that you rose from the grave. I also believe that you now sit in heaven on the right side of the Father, making intersession for me. I accept you as my Lord and my Savior.**"

Now that you have confessed with your mouth that Jesus is the son of God and that He died for our sins and rose from the grave, **YOU ARE NOW SAVED!!!!** You will spend your eternity in heaven.

The next step is very important- you must find a Bible-based church that teaches the word of God and confesses the Lord Jesus Christ to be the son of God. Don't delay. Do this immediately. Do not leave yourself open to the enemy. Get connected with the saints of the Most High God and keep yourself covered with the unspotted blood of the lamb.

Here is my prayer for you.

Father God,

I thank you for the opportunity to minister your word to the unsaved, the unchurched, and the uncommitted. Father God, I pray now for the souls who have just received the gift of salvation. Lord Father, they have opened their hearts to you, and I know that you have received them into your kingdom and written their names in the Book of Life. Father God, I pray that you will touch their lives and show yourself mightily before them. Let their eyes be opened by the scales falling off, allowing them to see clearly.

Father God, I even pray for the backslider, those who have turned away from you after receiving the gift of salvation. You said in your word that you desire that none would perish. So Lord, I send your word to them right now praying that they would confess the iniquity in their heart, repent, and turn from their evil ways, so that they may receive a life of abundance. You said in your word in Matthew Chapter 14, that every knee shall bow before you and every tongue will confess that Jesus is Lord.

Father God, I pray now that we all come under subjection to your word and that we will humbly submit our lives to you. I ask all these things in the name of my Lord and Savior Jesus Christ.

Amen, Amen, Amen!!!!

I will continue to pray for your success in your walk with God. Remember, this spiritual walk that you are about to embark on will not be an easy walk, but remember, the race is not given to the swift but to those who endure to the end.

Be blessed with heaven's best. I love you!

About the Editor

Dr. Cassundra White-Elliott resides in California with her family, where as an English/Education professor she works for various community colleges and universities.

When writing, she writes with the direction of the Holy Spirit, in an effort to share with God's people all that He has for them.

In addition to teaching and writing, Dr. White-Elliott also serves as an evangelistic teacher. She is also the founder of International Women's Commission, a ministry that serves the needs of the entire person, by attending to healing the mind, body, soul, and spirit.

Dr. White-Elliott holds a Ph.D. in Education, a Master's in English Composition, and a Bachelor's in Education.

Dr. White-Elliott is also the founder of CLF Publishing, LLC. For your publishing needs, go online to www.clfpublishing.org.

A Mother's Heart shares the unconditional love of mothers through a compilation of testimonies. Each testimony serves as a tribute to a special mother. The children of the represented mothers have lovingly written about their childhood, young adult life and/or older adult experiences they shared with their mother. As you read the writers' reflections, you will feel the expressions of love exude from the pages.

The purpose of this book is two-fold. First, it honors those mothers who stood by their children through the trials of life and showered them with unconditional love. Second, the book is a source of encouragement for mothers who may feel inadequate and question whether or not they are actually suited for motherhood. Our advice to mothers is, *"Be encouraged; the journey of motherhood may seem daunting at times and you may shed some tears, but your children will never forget the love you have shown them and instilled in them to share with others."*

Mothers may not be perfect, but they are definitely unmatched by any other category of person on God's green earth!

A Mother's Heart II shares the unconditional love of mothers through a compilation of testimonies. Each testimony serves as a tribute to a special mother. The children of the represented mothers have lovingly written about their childhood, young adult life and/or older adult experiences they shared with their mother. As you read the writers' reflections, you will feel the expressions of love exude from the pages.

The purpose of this book is two-fold. First, it honors those mothers who stood by their children through the trials of life and showered them with unconditional love. Second, the book is a source of encouragement for mothers who may feel inadequate and question whether or not they are actually suited for motherhood. Our advice to mothers is, "*Be encouraged; the journey of motherhood may seem daunting at times and you may shed some tears, but your children will never forget the love you have shown them and instilled in them to share with others.*"

Mothers may not be perfect, but they are definitely unmatched by any other category of person on God's green earth!

The following authors are included in this compilation:
Edwin Baltierra, Shelia Bryant-Colbert, Jean Cedeno,
Ilse Guadalupe Hernandez, Haley Keil, Haley King, Johnathon Lopez,
Ronnette Moore, Allyson Marie Sanders, Lucas van den Elzen,
Daron C. White, Ashton Wilson, Jessica Yslas, and Vanessa Zavala

CLF Publishing, LLC.
www.clfpublishing.org

Dr. Cassundra White-Elliott's books are available at:
www.creativemindsbookstore.com
www.amazon.com
www.barnesandnoble.com

A Mother's Heart III shares the unconditional love of mothers through a compilation of testimonies. Each testimony serves as a tribute to a special mother. The children of the represented mothers have lovingly written about their childhood, young adult life and/or older adult experiences they shared with their mother. As you read the writers' reflections, you will feel the expressions of love exude from the pages.

The purpose of this book is two-fold. First, it honors those mothers who stood by their children through the trials of life and showered them with unconditional love. Second, the book is a source of encouragement for mothers who may feel inadequate and question whether or not they are actually suited for motherhood.

Our advice to mothers is, "Be encouraged; the journey of motherhood may seem daunting at times and you may shed some tears, but your children will never forget the love you have shown them and instilled in them to share with others." Mothers may not be perfect, but they are definitely unmatched by any other category of person on God's green earth!

The following authors are included in this compilation:
Yolanda Castro, Georgette Usi, Isaac Thompson, Nicholas Harrison, Justin Harrison, Ashleigh Morris, Jerry G. Martin, Jourdan Jovel, Khalil Flemister, Audrey Albrecht, Cathy Vines-Nichols, Akayla Clayton, Dalejuan Jackson, Quantanique Williams, Millicent Redd, Ahleeyah Nichols, Julia Lary, Maria Guzman, Tyler Kowalski-Foley, Haley Keil, Fernando Lescano, Elaine M. Tolentino, and Karen Ruiz.

CLF Publishing, LLC.
www.clfpublishing.org

ISBN 978-1-945102-16-5

Dr. Cassundra White-Elliott's books are available at:
www.creativemindsbookstore.com
www.amazon.com
www.barnesandnoble.com

www.ingramcontent.com/pod-product-compliance
Lightning Source LLC
Chambersburg PA
CBHW070542170426
43200CB00011B/2522